ENGLISH

The Origins, History and
Development of the Language

ENGLISH

The Origins, History and
Development of the Language

Katharine Watson

St James Publishing

First published in 2000 as 'The Story of English'.
This edition published in 2002 by
St James Publishing
c/o St James Independent Schools
Earsby Street
London W14 8SH

Tel: 0870 870 8797   Fax: 0870 870 8798
email: stjamespublishing@stjamesschools.co.uk

Printed by Alden Press

Cover design by DL Designs
Text design by Joanna Turner
Map by Peter Bull Associates

ISBN 1-903843-12-X

A record for this book is available from the Britsh Library

Contents

Acknowledgements

The author wishes to thank Arthur Farndell, Monica Lacey and the editors at St James Publishing for their generous help and encouragement.

The publisher gratefully acknowledges permission to reprint extracts and adaptations from the following works:

1–2   *The Tao of Physics* by Fritjof Capra, published by Harper Collins Publishers Ltd.

7   Adapted from 'The Language Museum' in *The Mother Tongue* by Lancelot Hogben, published by Secker & Warburg.

12   *A Celtic Miscellany*, translated by K.H. Jackson, published by Routledge.

30–3   *The Magician's Nephew* by C.S. Lewis copyright © C.S. Lewis Pte. Ltd. 1955. Extract reprinted with permission.

33–4   *Siddartha* by Herman Hesse, published by Peter Owen Ltd., London.

34–6   *Notes on the Art of Poetry* by Dylan Thomas, published by J.M. Dent. With thanks also to Jeff Towns of Dylans Bookstore, Swansea (www.dylans.com).

37   *The Geeta* translated by Shri Purohit Swami, published by Faber & Faber Ltd.

38   *The Odyssey* by Homer, translated by E.V. Rieu, Penguin Classics, 1946, p25. Copyright © the Estate of E.V. Rieu , 1946. Reproduced by permission of Penguin Books Ltd.

39–40   *The Aeneid* by Virgil, translated by W.F. Jackson-Knight, Penguin Classics, 1956. Copyright © G.R. Wilson-Knight, 1956. Reproduced by permission of Penguin Books Ltd.

51–2   *The Telephone Call* by Dorothy Parker, from 'The Best of Dorothy Parker' by permission of Gerald Duckworth & Co. Ltd.

52–3   *Oleanna* by David Mamet, by permission of Methuen Publishing Ltd.

53–4   *Are Men The New Women?*, reprinted by permission of Dylan Jones and GQ Magazine.

Introduction

Children from a very early age naturally love language. You can hear them playing with sounds, trying out new words and phrases, repeating them over and over again, delighting in their sound and rhythm. If this love is nourished by the adults around them, through play and talk and reading of stories, and later on at school through learning to write their thoughts and create word pictures, poems and stories of their own, while at the same time being encouraged to explore an ever widening range of literature, it can grow into a life-long love affair. This is certainly what happened in my case. But it was not until, as a student at university, I was introduced to the history of the English language that I discovered what a fascinating and wonderful story it is. A little later I found myself giving lectures on the subject to various groups of adults, and was surprised and moved by the degree of interest and enthusiasm with which these talks were received. At around the same time the new National Curriculum for Schools began to demand that children at secondary school be taught about the history and development of English. I started to think that my own pupils might find the story of our language just as fascinating as the adults did. Most available textbooks at that time, however, dealt with the topic only in a very perfunctory manner. So I decided to tell my pupils the story myself. And that is how the present book was born.

The book is primarily designed as a stand-alone course for use in the classroom, which might take up a lesson a week for one term, and is suitable for pupils between the ages of 12 and 14 – i.e. in Years 8 or 9. At the end of each section there are suggestions for practical exercises, and the Appendix provides a range of illustrative material.

In its first edition, the book has been in use for some while within St James Schools, where I teach. The aim and intention of this new edition is to allow the book to reach a wider readership, both in its primary function as a teaching aid for schools, and also as a book of interest to the general reader. It was necessary to modify surprisingly little of the original content of the adult lectures, and so the book will perhaps also appeal to the adult reader with an interest in the subject. For those wishing to explore it in more depth, there is a select list of suggested further reading on the following page.

Since hearing the sound of the language in its various stages is crucial to an appreciation of its spirit, readers may be interested to know that an audiotape is available (price £5 on request from the publishers), which contains readings in the original languages from extracts of Sanskrit, Greek, Latin, Anglo-Saxon and Middle English, together with modern English translations of each passage.

Katherine Watson
March 2002

Further Reading

A.C. Baugh, *A History of the English Language* (1959)

B.M.H. Strang, *A History of English* (1970)

Otto Jespersen, *The Growth and Structure of the English Language* (1938)

G.H. McKnight, *The Evolution of the English Language* (1970)

W.F. Bolton, *The English Language – Essays by English and American Men of Letters 1490–1839* (1973)

Lancelot Hogben, *The Mother Tongue* (1964)

Steven Pinker, *The Language Instinct* (1994)

The Language Families of the World

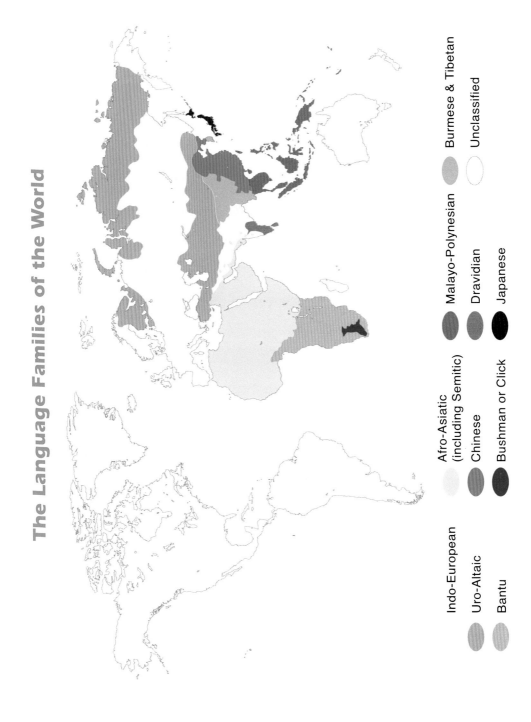

Indo-European

Uro-Altaic

Bantu

Afro-Asiatic (including Semitic)

Chinese

Bushman or Click

Malayo-Polynesian

Dravidian

Japanese

Burmese & Tibetan

Unclassified

1. The Beginning

Where does language come from? How did it begin? Nobody really knows. Some say it is the gift of the gods...

According to ancient belief, language came first, before anything else; and the universe itself was created by means of sound. That is to say, the Supreme Being spoke – or sang, or in some way set humming – a primeval Word or Original Sound, and from that the whole universe came into being.

We find this idea expressed in many different cultures. Most famously, in the Bible, the gospel of St. John opens with the statement:

> In the beginning was the Word. And the Word was with God, and the Word was God.

The Upanishads, from ancient India, also say:

> All this universe is the word OM; past, present, future – everything is OM.
> ... All this truly is God.

The account of the creation of the universe from the biblical Old Testament tells us that God said, "Let there be light." The ancient Egyptians also believed that God (in their view the Sun-god) sang, creating the world with a 'cry of light'. So did the Aztecs, the ancient people who once lived in what we call South America. So did the Australian Aborigines; even today, going 'walkabout', they find their way through the vast Australian bush by means of the Song-lines – ancient tracks which the Ancestors first sang into existence – which can still, according to today's Aborigines, be followed by listening to them and singing them.

There are also many legends concerning the gift of speech to Man. The Bible tells of Adam, the first man, being instructed to give names to all the things that God has created. Indian mythology speaks of the Dance of the Lord Shiva, according to which, as he danced his great cosmic dance, the sounds of the alphabet fell from Shiva's footsteps. Like all ancient legends, this is not meant to be taken literally; it expresses, in the form of a story, an idea about the true nature of creation. One modern scientist describes how, in a moment of insight, the legend of the Dance of Shiva came alive for him:

> I was sitting by the ocean one late summer afternoon, watching the waves rolling in and feeling the rhythm of my breathing, when I suddenly become aware of my whole environment as being engaged in a gigantic cosmic dance. Being a physicist, I knew that the sand, rocks, water and air around me were made of vibrating molecules and atoms, and that these consisted

of particles which interacted with one another by creating and destroying other particles. I knew also that the Earth's atmosphere was constantly bombarded by showers of 'cosmic rays', particles of high energy undergoing multiple collisions as they penetrated the air. All this was familiar to me from my research in high-energy physics, but until that moment I had only experienced it through graphs, diagrams and mathematical theories. As I sat on that beach my former experience came to life; I 'saw' cascades of energy coming from outer space, in which particles were created and destroyed in rhythmic pulses; I 'saw' the atoms of the elements and those of my body participating in this cosmic dance of energy; I felt its rhythm and I 'heard' its sound, and at that moment I knew that this was the Dance of Shiva, the Lord of Dancers worshipped by the Hindus.

(From *The Tao of Physics* by Fritjof Capra)

What we believe about speech and language depends upon what we think about Man and his relationship to the universe. Thus there is a quite opposite view, commonly held in the West, to the ancient one I have been describing. According to this, the earliest men gradually developed speech from primitive animal noises, progressing little by little from grunts to simple words for everyday things, until a day came when the first sentence, the first complete thought expressed in words, was uttered – probably something like, "I'm hungry," or "What's for dinner?"

More recently, cognitive neuro-scientists (people who study how the brain works, and how we think and know things) have shown that language is inherent in human beings – we are born with a capacity for language, inbuilt. What language we will actually speak of course depends on the language our parents speak – we learn by imitating them. But the young baby already has a built-in sense of grammar, and once it has learnt enough single words to begin trying to form whole statements or sentences, it will quite naturally structure them according to the basic laws of grammar. Another interesting idea recently put forward, which happens to accord exactly with what ancient Indian writings say, is that we do not think in English, or French, or Japanese, or whatever language we use; we think in a kind of 'mentalese', a language of the mind, which our brains then 'translate' for us into our spoken language. In fact, recent research rather tends to confirm the view expressed by some Indian philosophers that "Language came with the creation", or in other words that it is there from the beginning, just as St John says.

Whatever we think about the origin and purpose of language, one thing is certain: language does create. A writer or poet can create for us a whole world of the imagination, quite different from the one in which we spend our daily lives. And although we may not notice it, we ourselves create the kind of world we live in according to the words we carry in our minds. Thus the person who always tells himself or herself: "I am stupid," or "I am miserable," very soon becomes these things; whereas a person who thinks "I am happy," will certainly be so. Language bestows enormous power. To those around us, we may speak words of comfort, courage, inspiration and love; and if the words truly come from the heart, they will give these precious gifts to those for whom we speak. Words may begin a quarrel, or start a war; order a garden shed, or build a city; freeze and limit the heart and mind, or open and liberate them. As the Russian writer Alexander Solzhenitsyn once wrote, "One word of truth can change the whole world."

Practical Exercises

Discuss the ideas put forward in this chapter in class. Pupils may have observation and experience of their own to contribute.

What does the idea, 'Language is creative' mean to them in practice? What have they noticed about using a different language from English – what is the effect on the mind and emotions? What have they discovered about the effect on themselves or others of words (such as "I am stupid, clever, no good at..." etc.) held in the mind? Can they think of moments in history when someone's words have had powerful effects? Can words really be 'taken back'?

If there is time, read some of the relevant extracts from On Language *(Appendix A).*

2. Language Families

Another idea which turns up in ancient myths and legends – notably in the biblical story of the Tower of Babel – is that originally there was only one language, spoken by all people on earth – and indeed all creatures. However that may be, today there are in the world nearly three thousand different languages.

Fortunately for those who study the science of language, most languages in the world fall into one or other of a fairly small number of language groups, or families. Each family of languages is so called because the languages in the group seem to have descended from a common parent language.

One has to appreciate that languages change all the time – some very fast, some more slowly, depending on the circumstances. Even today, when language tends to be standardised through books, newspapers, radio and television, the English spoken by most young people in Britain is different in many ways from that spoken by their grandparents. It is even more different from the English spoken a couple of hundred years ago, and very different indeed from the English of Shakespeare's day. If we go back still further, to the fourteenth century and the language of Chaucer, we are likely to find the English very difficult to understand – at least at first sight. Three centuries before that – before the Norman Conquest – and English looks and sounds like a foreign language. Thus it is not difficult to understand how two tribes, say, who originally spoke the same language, but have moved apart and over the centuries become separated – perhaps by a great mountain range – may in time cease to understand one another's speech and may in effect be speaking two different languages. Yet a student of language would very quickly be able to tell that the two languages were in fact close relatives.

The main language families of the world are as follows:

1. Indo-European   This includes English, and most of the languages of Europe and of India, plus the Persian (or Iranian) language.

2. Semitic   Includes Arabic, Abyssinian, Assyrian, Hebrew, Maltese and Ethiopic – plus the now extinct languages of Aramaic (in which much of the Bible was originally written) and Phoenician.

3. Hamitic   Includes Coptic Egyptian, Berber, and various languages of North and Equatorial Africa.

4. Language groups of black Africa	These fall into three groups: **Sudanese**: from North Africa down to the equator **Bantu**: from the equator southwards – including Swahili and Xosa **Hottentot and Bushman**: extreme south.
5. Dravidian	The languages of South India, such as Tamil.
6. Indo-Chinese	Includes Cantonese and Mandarin Chinese, Tibetan, Burmese and Thai.
7. Malay-Polynesian	Languages spoken in the islands of the Indian and Pacific oceans, such as Fiji and Tahiti, and that of the Maoris of New Zealand.
8. Papuan	Languages of New Guinea and neighbouring islands
9. Australian Aborigine	
10. North American Indian	
11. Eskimo	
12. Ural-Altaic	(Ural) Finnish, Estonian, Livonian, Lappish, Hungarian (Altaic) Ottoman, Turkish, Turkestan, Mongolian, Manchu, Korean – and possibly Japanese, although some linguists put Japanese in a group all by itself.

The oldest language in Europe is Basque, which is not related to any other language. The Basque people, who live in the south west corner of France and along the north west border of Spain, are the oldest Western race. Their language, of which they are fiercely proud, is spoken by half a million people, and sounds utterly different from any other European language.

The map at the beginning of the book shows roughly how the main language groups are distributed around the world.

The Indo-European family of languages, of which English is a member, can also be divided into distinct groups or branches, as follows:

Indo-Iranian	Sanskrit, Prakrit languages of India (Parsi, Bengali, Hindi, Urdu), Romany (the language of gypsies), Persian and Avestan (the sacred Persian language).
Armenian, Albanian	These two have a mixed word stock, partially Indo-European, partially other languages.
Balto-Slavic	Lithuanian, Latvian, Prussian, Russian, Ukrainian, Byelorussian, Polish, Czech, Slovak, Serbian, Bulgarian, Croatian, Slovenian.
Hellenic	Greek – koine (literary) and demotic (popular).
Italic	Italian, Spanish, Portuguese, French, Romanian, Provencal, Walloon. (These are also known as the Romance languages.)
Celtic	Welsh, Breton, Cornish, Pictish, Gaelic (Scots and Irish). These languages were, before Christian times, spoken over the greater part of central and western Europe.
Germanic	East Germanic – Gothic (now extinct) North Germanic – Danish, Swedish, Norwegian, Icelandic, Faroese West Germanic – High German, Low German, Dutch, Flemish, Frisian – and last but not at all least – English.

All these Indo-European languages descend from a common parent language. Some say that this parent language is Sanskrit, the ancient language of India, which is claimed by some to be the oldest language in the world, although Western scholars think there must have been an even older language (which they call by the rather inelegant name of 'proto-Indo-European') from which Sanskrit itself derived.

Let's look now at some of the family likenesses between words in the different languages of the Indo-European family. Take a look at the following diagram.

Modern English	*mother*	*father*	*two*	*three*	*sun*
Sanskrit	*matri*	*pitri*	*dvi*	*tri*	*surya*
Greek	*mater*	*pater*	*due*	*treis*	*helios*
Latin	*mater*	*pater*	*duo*	*tres*	*sol*
Dutch	*moeder*	*vader*	*twee*	*drie*	*zon*
German	*Mutter*	*Vater*	*zwei*	*drei*	*sonne*
Swedish	*moder*	*fader*	*tva*	*tre*	*sol*
Danish	*moder*	*fader*	*to*	*tre*	*sol*
French	*mère*	*père*	*deux*	*trois*	*soleil*
Portuguese	*mae*	*pai*	*dois*	*tres*	*sol*
Spanish	*madre*	*padre*	*dos*	*tres*	*sol*
Italian	*madre*	*padre*	*due*	*tre*	*sole*
Welsh	*mam*	*tad*	*dau*	*tri*	*haul*
Cornish	*mam*	*tad*	*deu*	*try*	*houl*
Breton	*mamm*	*tas*	*deu*	*tri*	*heol*
Gaelic	*mathair*	*athair*	*da*	*tri*	*grian*
Old English	*moder*	*fæder*	*twa*	*thri*	*sunne*

Grimm's Law, or the Great Germanic Sound Shift

During the first half of the 19th century, the language scholar Jacob Grimm (one of the brothers Grimm, better known as the collectors of Grimm's Fairy Tales) observed that there is a regular 'sound shift' between the ancient classical languages – Sanskrit, Greek, Latin – and the Germanic branch of the Indo-European family (German, Dutch, English etc.). He noticed that where the classical languages have a *t* sound, the Germanic ones have *th*; classical *p* has changed to *f*; and classical *k* (or *c*) has changed to Germanic *h*.

Thus:

Sanskrit	Greek	Latin	Germanic
त	τ	t	þ
तृ	τρεισ	tres	three
प	π	p	f
पितृ	πατερ	pater	father
		pisces	fish
क	κ	c	h
हृद़	καρδια	cor	heart
		centum	hundred
व	φ	f	b
भर्ति	φερο	fero	bear

If you look again at the 'family likeness' chart, you will see that the Romance languages, French, Spanish, Portuguese, Italian, follow the classical sound, and the Germanic ones have changed. So words which at first sight may seem quite far apart, such as Latin *cor*, French *coeur*, and modern English *heart*, (Old English *heort*) – are more similar than we usually realise.

Practical Exercises

Using an etymological dictionary, look up some of these words and find out what is their origin (i.e. what language do they originally come from?). Also notice whether the word has changed its meaning since it first entered the English language.

abbreviate, amaze, biography, bread, calligraphy, cat, catastrophe, defend, deity, domestic, eat, eradicate, fairy, god, gospel, human, hooligan, hypocrisy, intelligent, jelly, kaleidoscope, knight, know, ladle, library, mother, museum, navigate, nice, obnoxious, O.K., pagoda, pandemonium, pansy, philosophy, quick, radiant, rage, read, refuge, sanity, science, school, smack, skill, starve, stupid, subterranean, suicide, summer, supervise, technology, term, theology, think, Thursday, tourist, town, train, transmutation, twinge, ugly, ultimate, utter, vague, vanquish, viaduct, vivid, wake, watch, weapon, yolk, young.

3. The Ancient Languages

A language remains a living tongue as long as there are people who use it for their daily speech. From time to time it happens that fewer and fewer people speak a particular language, until eventually it dies out. This has happened, for instance, to Cornish. There are no longer any people who speak Cornish as their native language.

There are certain languages, however, which, although they are no longer spoken as a living tongue, are nonetheless extremely important to us today. A language becomes great and important because great and important thoughts have been expressed in it, and the people who use it have become a great people. This may occur for a variety of reasons. A people may, for instance, acquire importance as a great trading nation, or as builders of an empire; or they may be great lawgivers; or have among them great thinkers, or great artists or poets. And their language and culture may continue to exert a powerful influence for centuries – even millennia.

Among the ancient languages which still influence us today are Sanskrit, Greek and Latin.

Sanskrit is important, not only because it is the mother of all the Indo-European family of languages (of which English is a member), but also because of the vast body of literature contained in it – including, for example, the two great Indian epics, *The Mahabharata* and *The Ramayana*; the beautiful and mysterious spiritual poems known as the *Upanishads*; and India's spiritual classic, *The Bhagavad Gita*. Although these works have only relatively recently become widely known in the West, their influence has spread throughout the Western world. Today there is increasing interest in these very ancient and profound writings.

Ancient Greek has had a much more obvious and direct influence upon us. Greece gave us Homer's epic poems, *The Iliad* and *The Odyssey*. *The Iliad* tells the story of the Trojan War, and *The Odyssey* recounts the adventures of one man, Odysseus (also known in Latin as Ulysses), as he returns to his home after the end of the war with Troy. These stories have been the inspiration of writers and poets ever since. Then there are the Greek myths, with all their strange and wonderful stories of the immortal gods; they too have provided a vast storehouse of material for poets, writers and artists throughout the whole of Western culture. But ancient Greece has informed and shaped our thinking, right down to the present day, in a still more important way, through its great philosophers, especially Socrates, Plato and Aristotle. Our whole way of seeing, understanding and interpreting the world is largely founded upon their ideas. Until very recently, the whole of Western education and culture was based upon the study of the Greek and Roman classics, together with the Bible. It is only during the past hundred years that we have begun to move away from that long tradition.

The ancient Romans, whose language was **Latin**, took most of their ideas, and their mythology, and their artistic inspiration, from the Greeks. The Latin poet, Virgil, wrote his epic, *The Aeneid*, as a kind of imitation of Homer. It tells the story of Aeneas, sole survivor from the citadel of Troy, and how he journeys across the sea to found the city of Rome.

The Romans brought to Western culture an efficient system of government and law, and a civilised and ordered way of life, in which great emphasis was placed upon the concept of honour. They were in general engineers, builders, lawgivers and administrators, rather than thinkers, poets or artists. They also conquered and ruled a vast empire, which lasted six hundred years and stretched from the Sahara Desert in Africa to Hadrian's Wall in northern Britain.

With the spread of the Roman empire, Latin became the chief language of the civilised West. It was adopted as the language of the Roman Church, and since the Church was the centre of all learning, Latin also became the international language of scholars. Up until the 9th century AD, Latin was the only written language in general use in Western Europe, and it continued to be used as a literary language right up to the seventeenth century. In the Roman Catholic Church it remained until the second half of the twentieth century the language used for all church services.

Today, if we read the work of the great English poets and writers of the past, we find their works full of references to classical (i.e. Greek and Roman) stories, myths and ideas – as well as stories and ideas from the Bible. Unless we know at least something of these two great traditions – the classical and the biblical – not only do we inevitably miss a great deal of what the writers, poets and artists of the past have to offer, but also we cut ourselves off from our own rich heritage.

Practical Exercises

The class might begin by examining the three extracts – Sections 1, 2 and 3 of Appendix B and comparing the text and translations to see if they can identify some of the words.

4. The Celts and the Romans

Long, long before the people who were to become the English arrived – some say as long as 250 thousand years before – there had been men living in the islands we now call Britain. In fact, in the early Stone Age, Britain was not even an island. There was no English channel, and the land was joined on to the mainland of Europe. There are still traces to be found of the people of the Stone Age (up to 2000 BC), Bronze Age (up to 500 BC), and Iron Age (from around 500 BC). Stonehenge, for instance, was built some time around 1500 BC. But we know nothing of the languages spoken by the people of those very early times.

Over the millennia, there was a gradual migration of peoples, spreading out westwards across Europe. At some stage during the Bronze Age the **Celts** arrived in these islands. They are the people properly called British, or, if you like, ancient British. They are the ancestors of today's Welsh and Breton people, and also of the Cornish. The next wave of people who arrived across the sea drove them west and southwards into Wales and Cornwall. Some also fled across the sea to found a new Britain, known today as Brittany – and their language is Breton.

To the Celtic people belong the legends of King Arthur and Merlin, around which a great store of wonderful stories – the legends of King Arthur – grew up. There was in fact a real King Arthur, a British king who lived in the 5th century AD and fought against the invading English. But the Arthur of legend is a figure surrounded by romance and mystery, and tales of heroic deeds, brave knights and beautiful ladies. Merlin is the great prophet, seer and magician. According to some authorities, Britain was once known as 'Merlin's Precinct', and it seems possible that there was once in ancient times a real Merlin, perhaps a Druidic priest, who was the spiritual leader and teacher of his people, the guardian of culture and civilisation, of poetry and kingship.[1]

During the time of the Celts, the **Romans** arrived in Britain. In 55 BC Julius Caesar, landing on the British coast, made his famous thrasonical boast: "Veni, vidi, vici – I came, I saw, I conquered". In fact, the real conquest did not take place until 100 years later, in AD 43. The British fought against the conquerors. In AD 61 there was a major uprising led by the British queen, Boadicea. But the Romans stayed 400 years. They carried out a thorough Romanisation of their new colony, building roads, cities, temples and theatres, and they introduced their language and laws. During this time also, Christianity made its first appearance in Britain. But then the Roman Empire began to decline, and in AD 410 the legions were withdrawn. The Romans left, never to return.

---

1   In one legend, Merlin says of himself: "I was taken out of my true self; I was a spirit, and knew the history of people long past, and could foretell the future. I knew then the secrets of nature, bird flight, star wandering, and the way fish glide." (from *Vita Merlini*)

They left the Celts, who had perhaps grown used to a softer way of living under Roman rule (all those baths!), without protection from the fierce tribes of Picts and Scots who kept attacking from the north. The British king Vortigern unwisely invited the Jutes – fierce Germanic sea-raiders from Jutland across the water – to come over and help fight them off.

In 449 the Jutes arrived, liked it here, and showed no inclination to depart. They settled in Kent. Word must have spread and the Jutes were soon followed by further waves of invaders: the Angles, who came from South Denmark and landed along the east coast, in what is still today called East Anglia; and the Saxons, a warlike tribe named after their favoured weapon, the *seaxe*, a short sword or dagger. They had been living along the west coast of Germany, and they entered the country via the river Thames and spread out south and eastwards.

Gradually, the Celtic tribes were dispossessed and driven out, into Wales, Cornwall and over the sea to Brittany. They took their traditional stories with them, and so it happens that today we can often trace two different versions of the same story, one from the Welsh tradition and the other from the Breton.

Almost nothing of the Celtic language and culture survived in what was to become England. Certain place names remained – for example 'Avon' is the Celtic word for 'river'. But such Celtic civilisation and learning as may have been left was quickly wiped out. Christianity disappeared. The earliest English were barbarians.

Here is a modern English translation of an Irish Celtic poem from the 7th century. It describes something human beings have always dreamed of, in myth and poetry – the magical islands of an earthly paradise.

There is an island far away, around which the sea-horses glisten, flowing on their white course against its shining shore; four pillars support it.

It is a delight to the eye, the plain which the hosts frequent in triumphant ranks; coracle races against chariot in the plain south of Findargad.

Pillars of white bronze are under it, shining through aeons of beauty, a lovely land through the ages of the world, on which many flowers rain down.

There is a huge tree there with blossom, on which the birds call at the hours; it is their custom that they all call together in concert every hour.

Colours of every hue gleam throughout the soft familiar fields; ranged round the music, they are ever joyful in the plain south of Argadnel.

Weeping and treachery are unknown in the pleasant familiar land; there is no fierce harsh sound there, but sweet music striking the ear.

Without sorrow, without grief, without death, without any sickness, without weakness, that is the character of Emhain; such a marvel is rare.

5. Old English 449–1066

What kind of language did the sea-raiders bring with them? What we call Old English, or Anglo-Saxon, is a vigorous, flexible, expressive language which lends itself to poetic expression. Only a fragment of the treasury of poetry which must once have existed in the language has come down to us today. The language is rich in words for things which interested or concerned the people who spoke it. For example, there are a great many words meaning 'battle' e.g. *gefeaht*, *gūþ*, *heaðo*, *hild*, *ȝewin*. And there are no less than 24 simple words meaning 'sea': e.g. *brim*, *dēop*, *flōd*, *holm*, *lagu*, *sǣ*, *strēam*, *ȳð*. (See pronounciation guide on page 40.)

There are also a very large number of compound words, or kennings – that is, words made by putting two words together, which are often poetic and figurative. For example, words for the sea include *swanrād* (the swan's road), *hwælweg* (the whale's way), and *fiscesbæþ* (fish's bath). Then also the language is very rich in words for the cold, winter and snow. In old English poetry it always seems to be winter. Frost and hail beat down, gulls scream, gannets cry – and men struggle against the elements, enduring them as best they can. (It's interesting to note that the Norse hell is cold.) The poets wrote often about loneliness and exile, in '*þis lǣnan līf*' (this transitory life).

There are also many words for prince, or leader: e.g. *æþeling*, *frēa*, *dryhten*, *hlāford*. Loyalty to your lord, the atheling, the prince or leader of your clan, is all-important. Very high value is placed upon friendship – with the 'hearth-companions' alongside whom you fight in battle, shoulder to shoulder. A man should have courage, and stand fast, for no-one can change fate. The idea of fate – *wyrd* – is very important in Anglo-Saxon poetry. It means a man's destiny – what he has to face in life. The Anglo-Saxon people valued thinking, solitude, the man who 'sits apart in meditation', as one poet describes it.

There are a number of letters used in Anglo-Saxon which we no longer have. Ash (æ) which is pronounced 'a' as in 'hat'; thorn (þ), which is pronounced 'th'; yogh (ȝ), pronounced 'y' or 'g'; and eth (ð), pronounced 'th'.

On the next page are the first five lines of *The Wanderer*.

'Oft him ānhaga	āre gebīdeð
Often the solitary one	*longs for grace,*
Metudes miltse	þēah þe hē mōdcearig
Maker's mercy	*yet troubled in mind*
geond lagulāde	longe sceolde
through the sea's tract	*he must for long*
hrēran mid hondum	hrīmcealde sǣ,
stir with hands	*the ice-cold sea,*
wadan wræclāstas:	wyrd bið ful ārǣd.'
travel the paths of exile:	*wyrd is set fast.'*

There are 12 words in these five lines which are totally unfamiliar to us today. The Anglo-Saxon language is now more or less unintelligible unless you make a special study of it. This means that for most people, English literature begins in the 14th century with Chaucer – or increasingly, not even that. Quite a number of university courses ignore everything before the 16th century and Shakespeare. It seems a shame, because it means that in terms of language and literature we are cut off from our roots.

It takes a while to appreciate what a great loss all this means. With the Norman Conquest, the Anglo-Saxon nobility was virtually wiped out, and with it a whole culture. The Norman invaders imported a whole new vocabulary, which replaced the native one. We lost, for instance, the capacity of Old English to extend its vocabulary by means of kennings – those wonderfully expressive compound words. We may regret the loss of, for instance, words like *ferðloca* – spirit house (i.e. heart), *hordcofan* – heart's treasure, *mōdgeþanc* – heart's thought, *līf-hūs* – life house (i.e. body). They seem so apt and direct.

The Conversion

In AD 597 an event took place which was to have an enormous impact on the language. St Augustine, sent by Pope Gregory in Rome, came to Britain and began to convert the English to Christianity. This of course brought a great influx of new ideas and new vocabulary to express them. Most of the words came from Latin, which was of course the language of the Church. But sometimes Anglo-Saxon words were adapted, or new words were formed, to describe the new ideas, and give it a new extended meaning. For example:

tungol-wītega – a man learned in stars: in other words a Magi
sundor-hālga – one who is holy and keeps himself apart: a Pharisee
ānsetla – an alone-sitter: a hermit

Þrynes – much nicer than 'Trinity'
leorning-cniht – a disciple

The study of Latin opened the way to Latin and Greek civilisation and culture. During the 8th century England became a great centre of learning and culture, with the schools at Wearmouth, Jarrow, Canterbury and Malmesbury. So we get some wonderful new words, such as:

stæf-cræft – letter-craft: in other words grammar
flit-cræft – dispute (flyting): logic
tungol-gescēad – star-reason: astronomy
eorþ-gemet – earth measure: geometry
sōn-cræft – sound craft: music
drēam-cræft – joy craft: music

Gradually the Latin words took over from these first, fresh, delightful native responses.

There was great reverence for the Latin terms used by the new religion, and respect for the authority of the church. Also there was a desire for precision and uniformity, which led to a kind of intellectual snobbery. People felt that using Latin gave them higher status. Many new Latin words entered the language during this period. We wouldn't think of them as 'foreign' now. Words like, *monk*, *abbot*, *prior*, *apostle*, *cell*, *cloister*, *collect*, *creed*, *prophet*. Little by little these words replaced the old Anglo-Saxon ones.

So the first wave of new words and ideas came into the language on the tide of Christianity – and it was a Latin wave. The next wave was very different.

The Vikings

In AD 793 began a series of plundering raids by the Viking Norsemen which continued in sporadic bursts, culminating in the years between 1016 and 1050, when England was under Danish rule, as first King Svein and then King Cnut reigned. (Cnut is better known as King Canute, well known to children as the king who sat on the beach and commanded the tide not to rise.)

The Norsemen were fierce fighting men of a practical spirit, with, it seems, a peculiar talent for law and administration. In fact we owe our word *law* to them. They brought with them words for warfare and for legal matters – most of which disappeared again when the Normans arrived. Only 40 words now survive.

Many of the words the Scandinavians brought were terms for the most ordinary, everyday things such as *bread* or *eggs*. The two languages – the Anglo-Saxon and the Scandinavian – were anyway very similar. For example, they had identical words for man, wife, father, mother, thing, life, sorrow, winter. Sometimes there are pairs of words (doublets) that originally meant the same thing, but have since moved apart in Modern English, acquiring slightly different meanings. For example:

Native	whole	no	shirt	rear	church	yard
Scandinavian	hale	nay	skirt	raise	kirk	garth

Perhaps just because the languages were so similar, one effect of the gradual mingling of the two, which happened naturally as the Viking invaders settled down and inter-married with the native population, was that the original endings of words in Anglo-Saxon (which used to have noun and verb endings, rather like Latin) were dropped, and the language became simpler.

Practical Exercises

The class could try translating Ælfric's Colloquy, *with the aid of the glossary provided. They could also attempt to speak some of the verse, beginning with* Cædmon's Hymn. *See Appendix B.*

16

6. The Middle English Period: The Normans

The next 'event' we have to consider is the Norman Conquest of AD 1066. This marks the beginning of the Middle English Period. The coming of the French-speaking Normans was truly cataclysmic in its effect on the English language.

The Scandinavian Vikings had been culturally on a par with the Anglo-Saxon English. The Normans, however, brought with them a superior culture – the culture of the Mediterranean, of Italy and France. At the same time the Normans were highly efficient and ruthless people. They carried out a thorough subjugation of the whole country. They had no interest in learning the language of the conquered people – no interest in their culture, customs or literature. They had their own ideas of law and government. They took over all positions in the Church and State. The Anglo-Saxon nobility was virtually wiped out. As a result English, which had been the official and literary language, in which an important and flourishing literature had been written, became merely the language of the serfs – a despised lower class of subject people. For nearly three centuries, almost all literature was written in Latin or French – Latin for serious affairs and for religious purposes, French for entertainment. The only exception was devotional and religious literature, especially that written for women and for simple, uneducated folk.

Meanwhile, the Norman conquerors retained their contacts in Normandy, where they owned large estates. The kings of England did not speak English at all, although Henry II (1154–1189) probably understood it. They continued to rule large parts of France, and to choose their wives from there. French was constantly being reinforced.

For three centuries, English and French existed side by side. In fact, English very nearly did not survive. If it had not been for the loss of Normandy in 1204, an event which forced the Normans to decide whether they wanted to stay as Frenchmen or finally become English, we might still be speaking French in this country today. (And so, therefore, might the citizens of America, Australia, Canada, New Zealand, South Africa and so on...)

At the beginning of the time of Norman rule the conquered English found themselves forced to learn enough of their new masters' language to understand them. One of the first words to enter English at this time was *prisun* – which tells us perhaps something of the kind of relationship between the two peoples. But with the constant stream of literature being written in French, French vocabulary took the English language by storm. There was a complete vocabulary change. Gradually the old words were forgotten, and the new ones took their place. Little by little, as the centuries wore on, the two peoples merged into one.

Knowledge of French, the upper class language, became a matter of prestige. Robert of Gloucester wrote that, "Unless a man knows French, he is considered of little account," while Higden reports that "oplondysch men" liked to be able to speak

French "for to be more ytold of". However, once the loss of Normandy had taken place, and the nobility had to decide to become English, they began to be more interested in the native language. Little by little English was re-established. In 1362, during the reign of Edward III, the Opening of Parliament was for the first time conducted in English, not French. Soon after that, the practice of pleading in English was established in the law courts. Gradually, under the influence particularly of Chaucer, poets began to write in English – poets like Langland, Gower, and the anonymous 'Gawain poet'. Suddenly it was considered the done thing to write in English.

But it was an English completely changed, in vocabulary and in spirit, wholly different in character, rhythm and feeling from the Anglo-Saxon. The literature was full of the influence of French and Italian romance literature, love poems, tales of King Arthur and his knights, stories of beautiful ladies and sighing lovers.

The French spoken in England "after the scole of Stratford-atte-Bowe", as Chaucer calls it, became despised. We can see roughly where English finally took over, for Higden, writing in the early 14th century, tells us that children did all their lessons in French. A century later, Trevisa translates Higden's words, and puts in a note to say that they are now taught in English. By the end of the fifteenth century, the fusion of the two languages was complete.

However, there must have been a fair bit of confusion while all this was taking place, as the following extract from Caxton (written in 1490) suggests:

And certaynly our langage now used varyeth ferre from that whiche was used and spoken whan I was borne. For we englysshe men ben borne under the domynacyon of the mone which is never stedfaste but ever waverynge, wexynge one season and waneth and decreaseth another season. And that comyn englysshe that is spoken in one shyre varyeth from a nother. In so moche that in my dayes happened that certayn marchauntes were in a shippe in tamyse for to have sayled over the see into zelande, and for lacke of wynde they taryed atte forlond, and wente for to refreshe them. And one of theym named sheffelde, a mercer, cam into an hows and axed for mete, and specyally he axyd after eggys. And the good wyf answerde that she coude speke no frenshe, And the marchaunt was angry, for he also coude speke no frenshe, but wolde haue hadde egges, and she understode hym not. And thenne at laste a nother sayd that he wolde haue eyren. Then the good wyf sayd that she understod hym wel. Lo what sholde a man in thyse dayes now wryte, egges or eyren? Certaynly it is harde to playse every man by cause of dyversite and chaunge of langage. For in these dayes every man that is in ony reputacyon in his countre wyll utter his communicacyon and maters in suche maners and terms that fewe men shall understonde theym.

In many cases the old English word survived alongside the newer borrowed words, so that we have many pairs of words in English whose meaning is similar, but which carry a subtly different emotional quality. For example:

| **Native** | *begin* | *freedom* | *child* | *happiness* | *friendly* | *hearty* | *house* |
| **French** | *commence* | *liberty* | *infant* | *felicity* | *amicable* | *cordial* | *mansion* |

The native words are vivid and homely, and carry an intimate emotional force. The French words are colder, more aloof, formal, dignified.

The new, or 'borrowed', words tended to come from a number of specific areas. Some examples:

Words to do with Government:
crown, reign, allegiance, exile, tyrant, authority, government.

Words related to Law:
adultery, fraud, evidence, inquest, heritage.

Words from Religion:
cardinal, hermitage, absolution, charity, devotion, virtue, religion.

Words related to War:
war, peace, army, lieutenant, besiege, conquer.

Words used at court and in society:
chivalry, courage, manners, courtesy; aunt, uncle, nephew, niece.

Words to do with trade:
butcher, grocer, tailor, money, price, value.

Household words:
boil, fry, roast, cream, sugar, banquet, feast, carpet, chair, table.

Words relating to the Arts:
rhyme, poem; cathedral, choir; arch, palace; painting, art, sculpture, colour, design; chant, chord, harmony; college, degree, university; fashion, dress, coat, embroidery, lace, satin, taffeta; diamond, emerald, pearl.

Finally, a miscellaneous group, relating perhaps to story-telling:
action, adventure, frank, gentle, tender; marriage; grief, folly, rage.

There were a number of different dialects spoken in different parts of the country: South, North Midland, South Midland, and North. Chaucer wrote in the South Midland dialect, which became the London Standard. There was, however, no such thing as 'Standard English' as we know it today. The idea of 'correct English' did not come until very much later. Nor was there any such thing as correct spelling. You spelt a word as it sounded; Chaucer often spells the same word one way in one line, and a different way two lines later. It was not until the introduction of the printing press – Caxton again – that spelling became standardised.

One effect of all this was to alter the way in which English extended its vocabulary. No longer, when a new word was needed for something, did the English create a new compound word, like the wonderful *kennings* of Anglo-Saxon, so vivid and easy to understand. Instead, they borrowed the new word from another language. This meant that ordinary people who did not have the advantage of a university education could no longer always understand words in their own language – a situation which was to become increasingly marked during the next period of change.

What did the new language we call Middle English look and sound like? Here is a description of the Wife of Bath from Chaucer's *Canterbury Tales*.

A good wyf was ther of bisyde Bathe,
But she was somdel deef, and that was scathe.   somdel: *slightly;* scathe: *a pity*
Of clooth-makyng she hadde swich an haunt,   haunt: *talent*
She passed hem of Ypres and of Gaunt.   hem: *them*
In al the parisshe wif ne was ther noon
That to th'offrynge bifore hire sholde goon;   offrynge: *church mass*
And if ther dide, certeyn so wrooth was she,
That she was out of alle charitee.
Hir coverchiefs ful fyne weren of ground;   *were of finest texture*
I dorste swere they weyeden ten pound
That on a Sonday weren upon hir heed.
Hir hosen weren of fyn scarlet reed,   hosen: *stockings*
Ful streite y-tyed, and shoos ful moiste and newe.
Bold was hire face, and fair, and reed of hewe.
She was a worthy womman al hir lyve;
Housebondes at chirche-dore she hadde fyve.

Practical Exercises

The class could also recite some of the Chaucer passages from the Middle English section of Appendix B. See the pronunciation guide on p. 48.

They might also attempt a translation of a few lines of Chaucer.

If there is time, compare the different dialects of Chaucer and the Gawain poet.
What makes the Gawain poet more difficult for us to understand?

7. The Renaissance: 16th and 17th Centuries

First of all, what is – or was – the Renaissance? The name means 're-birth'.

During the 14th and 15th centuries in Italy there took place a great revival of learning under the influence of Latin, and especially Greek, literature. Most exciting of all to the thinkers of the time was the re-discovery of the Greek philosopher Plato. During the medieval period the chief influences upon thought, art and literature had been on the one hand the Church, and on the other Aristotle. But the discovery of Plato seemed to open up a whole new world of ideas. For example, instead of seeing Man, as the Middle Ages had done, as an essentially weak and sinful creature whose purpose in life was to cultivate humility and devotion to God, while scorning earth and its pleasures so as to prepare himself for life after death, the Renaissance began to see Man as a reflection of God's glory, and Man's soul as divine. People began to cultivate the ideal of a 'universal man', a man whole and complete, proud of his godlike intellect, his strength, beauty and artistic power. It was, in effect, a totally new concept of Man and his relationship with life, nature and art. It produced a tremendous sense of excitement and inspiration. Man's possibilities suddenly seemed limitless. And it gave rise, particularly in 15th century Florence, to an astonishing flowering of art and literature, producing, above all, some of the greatest artists the world has known – men like Leonardo da Vinci, Michelangelo, Raphael and Donatello.

This great flourishing of ideas and of artistic endeavour gradually spread, during the 16th and 17th centuries, to the countries of northern Europe. It brought with it an enthusiasm for all things Greek, in art, architecture, literature and thought. There was an immense hunger and reverence for learning and the use of the mind; and a growing interest, too, in science, exploration and discovery.

The English Renaissance coincides with the reign of Elizabeth I. The flowering which took place in England has a number of elements. It was a great age for English music; it also saw the beginnings of scientific investigation; and with the discovery of the New World, the world itself seemed much larger, and opened up opportunities for seafaring adventure. The period is also notable for the advances made in the education of women – with Elizabeth herself a shining example. But most important of all was the great flourishing of English literature. Besides a host of great English writers, this is the age of Shakespeare.

The effect of all these new ideas and the 'new learning' upon the English language was very marked. New vocabulary poured into the language, this time not from French but from Latin and Greek. And the new words tended to be learned ones. A few examples:

genius, theory, enthusiasm, antithesis, catastrophe, criterion, benefit, emancipate, meditate, extravagant, insane, pathetic, pernicious...

The main areas of borrowing were law, education, medicine, alchemy, astronomy, and science generally. The number of words adopted was enormous – so much so that Thomas Browne complained, "We shall, within a few years, be fain to learn Latin to understand English." In fact, English took over a quarter of the entire Latin vocabulary.

It was a period of intense consciousness of language – a fact which is reflected in many of Shakespeare's plays, where he pokes gentle fun at characters like Dogberry in *Much Ado About Nothing*, Elbow in *Measure for Measure*, and Holofernes in *Love's Labours Lost*, who try, with comical results, to use the learned words they have heard without understanding their meaning. The men who, under the direction of Thomas Cranmer, compiled what was to become the first official prayer book of the Church of England (now known as the Book of Common Prayer) obviously recognised the difficulties people were under, and helpfully supplied pairs of synonyms, with a new 'learned' word alongside the old, unlearned one, so that people could understand the prayers. For example, the prayer book asks that the Queen may "vanquish and overcome" her enemies; that she may attain "joy and felicity"; that we may do what is "requisite and necessary" – and all this is addressed to a congregation who are "assembled and met together".

In time, a feeling grew that this wholesale invasion of the language by new, difficult and long words was going too far. This gave rise to what was termed the 'inkhorn controversy', in which the arguments raged, with much ink spilt on both sides, between those who deplored this influx of 'ink-horn terms', and those who praised the extravagance of the extremely ornate 'aureate style'. Fortunately, moderation evidently prevailed, and many of the new words had only a very short life in English. Among those which did not 'take' are the following:

Armipotent, discruciating, fatuate, lapidifical, obstupefact, vadimonial.

During this period also, or rather between the 14th and 16th centuries, there were important changes in the vowel sounds of English. In Chaucer's day, the letter 'i', as in *I speak, I laugh, I think* etc. would have been pronounced *ee*. Now it changes to *ay*, as in the modern pronunciation. Similarly, modern English *house* would have been pronounced *hoose*, but now *ou* changes its pronunciation to modern *ow*. And whereas Chaucer would have pronounced *me* like modern English *may*, and *day* like modern English *die*, over the period spanning the end of the Middle Ages and the beginning of the modern age, all these sounds took on more or less the sound they have in Standard English today. The result of all this, of course, is that the language sounds utterly different from the way it sounded in the Middle Ages.

But the most significant factor in this period from the point of view of language was a complete change in attitude. In the 300 years following the Norman Conquest English had been re-established for practical purposes, but this was only half the battle. English did not fully 'come of age' until the end of the 16th century.

During the 15th century we find Caxton – and indeed all writers – constantly apologising for the 'symple and rude englissh' as compared to the 'fayre langage of frensshe'. English was described again and again as rude, gross, barbarous, vile. It was seen as plain and serviceable enough for everyday purposes, but it lacked the sweetness, refinement and elegance of French, or the prestige and eloquence of the classical languages.

A language, then as now, is generally valued for what has been written in it – what is enshrined in it. People who had benefited from the new learning – men for instance like Thomas More and John Colet, founder of St Paul's School – felt a great sense of responsibility towards the ignorant. They took a keen interest in education, and there was a tremendous spate of translations of learned works from Latin and Greek into English. The decisive turning point in attitude to English came when the Bible was translated. English began to be seen as more worthy, and there was a gradual build-up of confidence in it. Thomas More indeed declared: "For as for that our tongue is called barbarous, it is but a fantasy; for so is, as every learned man knoweth, every strange language to other." Writers and poets laboured to improve and augment the language, and make it more 'copious'. During the last quarter of the 16th century there was a sudden great literary upsurge – and on the crest of it rode Shakespeare.

This changed everything. English was no longer seen as merely a practical instrument, but as a medium of free expression. Sir Philip Sidney wrote: "For the uttering sweetly and properly the conceit of the mind, which is the end of speech, that hath it equally with any tongue in the world." There was an uprush of creative enthusiasm and delight in the use of the language. Eloquence in English became an accomplished fact for all to see. There was a tremendous sense of excitement as people realised that English was capable of giving expression to the very finest thoughts. Richard Mulcaster, one of the stoutest champions of English, remarked, "I reverence the Latin, but I worship the English."

Thus it was that the English language, having gone through all these stages of refinement, was ready and waiting for the Authorized Version of the Bible and the works of William Shakespeare. These two represent the pinnacle of all that has ever been written in English, and seem unlikely to be surpassed in the foreseeable future.

Practical Exercises

Read some of the extracts from the Renaissance English section of Appendix B. Consider what elements make their language different from our own speech.

Pupils might work on this in pairs, discussing a given passage together, underlining the words and phrases they have picked out, and then explaining to the class how these differ from modern speech.

It might also be an interesting exercise to try to 'translate' a few lines into modern English, and then compare the two versions in terms of how they sound.

8. Modern English

The rest of the story is fairly simple.

There were some important changes in grammar. By the end of the 17th century, for example, the old 'do' forms (as in 'I that do speak a word may call it back') had been lost. On the whole, the difference was that alternative ways of expressing ideas were dropped, leaving less flexibility in some respects. For example:

In statements:

whereas Shakespeare could use either *I do think*, *he did speak* or *I think*, *he spoke*, today we have only the latter forms. *Do* is used only for emphasis, as in *I do hope this works*.

In forming questions:

In the 16th century, questions could be formed either by using *do – Does he laugh? Do you think?* – or by reversing the verb and pronoun – *Laughs he? Think you?* We have lost the second option.

In forming negatives:

Though it is still possible in modern English to say *I care not*, *I do not care* would be more usual, and we would be unlikely to say, *I sent it not*, or *Believe it not*. Instead we use *do – I did not send it. Do not believe it.*

The other important grammatical change is the gradual dying out of the thee/thou forms, and the -eth/-est endings that accompany them. They were retained, at least until fairly recently, only for the special purpose of religious worship. English, therefore, unlike some languages, does not make a distinction between familiar and formal forms of address (as with, for instance, French *tu* and *vous*).

During the 18th century people began to feel the need to regularise, order and classify language. In 1755 Johnson compiled the first English Dictionary, with its famous definition of *lexicographer* (one who compiles dictionaries) as 'a harmless drudge'. This was followed by a spate of attempts at writing English Grammars. Up to this point, there had never been a formal English grammar; the language had just grown and developed with the uses made of it. The first grammars were simply descriptive ones: attempts to classify and describe the language, in a systematic way, *as it is*. There soon followed, however, efforts at *prescriptive* grammars – rules and regulations setting out what is correct or incorrect. These early grammarians found their task difficult, because they tried to fit the English language into the same model as Greek and Latin grammars, for which it is not very well suited. Instead of analysing how the language actually behaves, they tried to lay down how it ought to behave. Recently, scholars and others have come to understand that it is the underlying structure and grammatical concepts that matter, rather than the form.

All this led, especially with the spread of the British Empire in the 19th century, to a great interest in the study of language as a whole – particularly oriental languages. This interest was not confined to Britain. Academics throughout Europe, and especially Germany, were seized with enthusiasm for this study. Western scholars discovered Sanskrit, and they explored and compared languages from all over the world, and gradually evolved the notion of 'language families' that we saw earlier. For a time, the realisation that so many languages were closely related to one another, and had evolved out of one another, led to the hope of finding, behind all languages, a single 'mother' language. However, by the 1930s the Nazi regime in Germany had taken over this idea and hitched it to their notion of a 'master race'. Consequently, the idea became disreputable, and scholars ceased to pursue it.

English continues to extend its vocabulary, borrowing freely whenever the need is felt. The expansion of the British Empire brought a whole new influx of words. For example:

From American Indians:
hickory, moccasin, papoose, squaw, toboggan, tomahawk, wigwam.

From Mexico, Cuba and the West Indies:
barbecue, buccaneer, cannibal, canoe, cayenne, chocolate, hammock, hurricane, potato, tobacco, tomato.

From India and the Far East:
bangle, bungalow, calico, cashmere, china, chintz, curry, dinghy, juggernaut, jungle, karma, mandarin, pundit, thug, toddy, veranda; gingham, indigo, mango, seersucker.

From Africa:
banana, boorish, chimpanzee, gorilla, guinea, palaver, voodoo, zebra.

From Australia:
boomerang, kangaroo, wombat, wallaby.

The 20th century has also seen a massive influx of new vocabulary from a number of different areas. In particular, the growth of science, and of many branches of science and medicine, has produced the need for hundreds, probably thousands of new specialist words. Most of these are new compounds formed from Greek and Latin roots. A very few examples must suffice:

electroscope, biochemical, stratosphere, psychoanalysis, radioactivity, nitro-glycerine, ultraviolet, arteriosclerosis, homeopathic, bacteriology – etc. etc.

In fact, many of the words we use almost daily – *television, telephone, aeroplane, cinema, microwave, video, computer* (and all the host of words to do with computer technology) were unknown before the 20th century.

The various wars and political strife in general have also brought with them a crop of new words or combinations of words:

tank, gas mask, camouflage, periscope, blackout, blitz, paratroop, jeep; iron curtain, nuclear fission, atom bomb, gulag, perestroika, glasnost, scud missile...

There has also been a proliferation of acronyms: NATO, UNICEF, AIDS, WAR, RADA, IRA...

Alongside all these imported or invented words, English has re-discovered its ability, especially in 'popular' speech, to coin new compound words or phrases. Thus we have: *take-away, blow-up, sit-in, out-take, stake-out, stir-fry, white-out, make-over, downsize* and a host of similar expressive terms.

Meanwhile, words already in the language continue, as they have always done, to change their meaning. An area of rapid change is the language of slang, especially among teenagers. Each generation seems to need new words to express the twin ideas: 'very good indeed' and 'very bad indeed'. Often their meanings are almost the opposite to what the word means in more conventional usage. Current examples at the time of writing are: *cool, wicked, sad*. Sometimes it becomes almost impossible to use the word in its conventional sense – as for example with the word *gay* – and a kind of gap is left where its original meaning – 'happy, light-hearted' – used to be. *Gay* is an example of a *euphemism* – that is a mild or pleasant sounding expression used in place of one which the speaker thinks too unpleasant, or too blunt, or too embarrassing. Other examples are, 'Are they sleeping together?', 'She passed away last night', and all the various words for 'lavatory' – which itself is a euphemism: it literally means 'a place for washing', from Latin *lavare*. (Death, and the two bodily functions of procreation and elimination are extremely rich fields when it comes to euphemisms.)

But the main form of semantic change is simply the gradual change of meaning that comes about over the years. If you look at any good etymological dictionary, you will find that a great many words have changed their meaning since they first entered the English language. A prime example is the word *nice*. It entered the language from Normandy in the 13th century when it meant 'foolish, stupid'. In the 14th century it came to mean 'wanton', in the 15th 'coy, shy'. In the 16th century it diversified its meaning to cover 'fastidious', 'dainty', 'difficult to manage or decide', 'minute and subtle', 'precise, critical', or 'minutely accurate, Shakespeare uses it in *Romeo and Juliet* to mean 'trivial'. We still use it, as in 'a nice distinction' to mean minute and subtle. Not until the 18th century did it take on the meaning most associated with it today: 'pleasant, agreeable'. Recently it seems to have acquired yet another meaning – something like 'tactless, inappropriate' – as in 'Nice one!' Most of the earlier meanings have been lost, and nowadays when we say that someone is 'nice' we don't – at least specifically – usually mean that they are foolish.

* * *

The English language will go on changing. It will go on taking on board new words to express new ideas and things. The sound will also continue to change. Anyone who listens to a radio broadcast from the 1940s or 50s cannot fail to notice how much more clipped the language sounded then. Now that language is continuously being recorded through television and radio, our descendants will be able to listen to our speech, and will no doubt find it funny and strange. In fact, we are currently going through a period of quite rapid change in English. What used to be called the 'King's English', or more recently 'Standard English', is increasingly giving way to what has been referred to as 'Estuary English', in which the vowels are flatter and less differentiated from one another (with a general tendency to move towards an 'ee' sound), and glottal stops frequently take the place of dental consonants. It is noticeable also that the language of, say, Dickens, is less accessible to young people than it was perhaps 40 years ago. In terms of written language, we also favour a much more informal style, with shorter and simpler sentences, than was the norm a century ago.

What is accepted as 'correct' is also changing and will continue to change. There is no real, fixed, 'correct' English. The idea is false. A language must change. You cannot just choose an arbitrary moment in the development of a language and say, 'Now, this is the perfect state of the language. This is correct.' All we can say is what is currently acceptable in good, educated usage.

Meanwhile, there are now many different forms of English, besides 'British English' and 'American English', being spoken all over the world – many of them with a flourishing literary tradition of their own. (It is, incidentally, important to recognise that all these different 'Englishes' are equally valid. What counts is what is being thought and spoken in them.) During the past half century there has been a great deal of cross-fertilisation among writers from India, Africa, the Caribbean, South America, the USA and Canada, as well as British authors, and many of the different ethnic groups within Britain are also producing their own contribution to literary culture.

At the same time, there is a tendency for languages and dialects to disappear. The influence of radio and television, and of fast, efficient travel has brought people together, so that, in language at least, there is a movement towards unity. English is now spoken either as a first or as a second language by a vast number of people all around the world. Of particular significance, perhaps, is the fact that English is the language of the internet and of the whole rapidly mushrooming world of electronic communication. This in itself is bound to have a huge impact on language and meaning. It has recently been predicted that within a relatively short time – perhaps even within the next hundred years – English will have become the universal language, spoken by all human beings everywhere on this planet.

The important question is – how is this language going to be used?

Practical Exercises

Discuss the ideas and information in this section. Pupils may have knowledge and experience of their own to contribute.

Read one or two of the extracts from the Modern English section of Appendix B, and consider what special characteristics make them different from earlier English. Look at both style and vocabulary. What is it that writers and speakers of English today can do which would not have been possible to people from earlier times?
The class could now attempt to formulate what they have learnt from this course by writing their own simplified history of the English Language.

Appendix A – On Language

Extract 1

Words, Words

"When *I* use a word," Humpty Dumpty said in rather a scornful tone, "it means just what I choose it to mean – neither more nor less."

"The question is," said Alice, "whether you can make words mean different things."

"The question is," said Humpty Dumpty, "which is to be master – that's all."

Alice was too much puzzled to say anything, so after a minute Humpty Dumpty began again. "They've a temper, some of them – particularly verbs, they're the proudest – adjectives you can do anything with, but not verbs – however, I can manage the whole lot! Impenetrability! That's what I say!"

"Would you tell me, please," said Alice, "what that means?"

"Now you talk like a reasonable child," said Humpty Dumpty, looking very much pleased. "I meant by 'impenetrability' that we've had enough of that subject, and it would be just as well if you'd mention what you mean to do next, as I suppose you don't intend to stop here all the rest of your life."

"That's a great deal to make one word mean," said Alice in a thoughtful tone.

"When I make a word do a lot of work like that," said Humpty Dumpty, "I always pay it extra."

"Oh!" said Alice. She was too much puzzled to make any other remark.

"Ah, you should see 'em come round me of a Saturday night," Humpty Dumpty went on, wagging his head gravely from side to side, "for to get their wages, you know."

(Alice didn't venture to ask what he paid them with; and so you see I can't tell *you*.)

from Alice Through the Looking Glass by Lewis Carroll

Extract 2

Narnia, Awake! – Creation through sound

"Hush!" said the Cabby. They all listened.

In the darkness something was happening at last. A voice had begun to sing. It was very far away and Digory found it hard to decide from what direction it was coming. Sometimes it seemed to come from all directions at once. Sometimes he almost thought it was coming out of the earth beneath them. Its lower notes were deep enough to be the voice of the earth herself. There were no words. There was hardly even a tune. But it was, beyond comparison, the most beautiful noise he had ever heard. It was so beautiful he could hardly bear it. The horse seemed to like it too: he gave the sort of whinny a horse would give if, after years of being a cab-horse, it found itself back in the old field where it had played as a foal, and saw someone whom it remembered and loved coming across the field to bring it a lump of sugar.

"Gawd!" said the Cabby. "Ain't it lovely?"

Then two wonders happened at the same moment. One was that the voice was suddenly joined by other voices; more voices than you could possibly count. They were in harmony with it, but far higher up the scale: cold, tingling, silvery voices. The second wonder was that the blackness overhead, all at once, was blazing with stars. They didn't come out gently one by one, as they do on a summer evening. One moment there had been nothing but darkness; next moment a thousand, thousand points of light leaped out – single stars, constellations, and planets, brighter and bigger than any in our world. There were no clouds. The new stars and the new voices began at exactly the same time. If you had seen and heard it, as Digory did, you would have felt quite certain that it was the stars themselves which were singing, and that it was the First Voice, the deep one, which had made them appear and made them sing.

"Glory be!" said the Cabby, "I'd ha' been a better man all my life if I'd known there were things like this."

The Voice on the earth was now louder and more triumphant; but the voices in the sky, after singing loudly with it for a time, began to get fainter. And now something else was happening.

Far away, and down near the horizon, the sky began to turn grey. A light wind, very fresh, began to stir. The sky, in that one place, grew slowly and steadily paler. You could see shapes of hills standing up dark against it. All the time the Voice went on singing.

There was soon light enough for them to see one another's faces. The Cabby and the two children had open mouths and shining eyes; they were drinking in the sound, and they looked as if it reminded them of something. Uncle Andrew's mouth was open too, but not open with joy. He looked more as if his chin had simply dropped away from the rest of his face. His shoulders were stooped and his knees shook. He was not liking the Voice. If he could have got away from it by creeping into a rat's hole, he would have done so. But the Witch looked as if, in a way, she understood the music better than any of them. Her mouth was shut, her lips were pressed together, and her fists were clenched. Ever since the song began she had felt that this whole world was filled with a Magic different from hers and stronger. She hated it.

The eastern sky changed from white to pink and from pink to gold. The Voice rose and rose, till all the air was shaking with it. And just as it swelled to the mightiest and most glorious sound it had yet produced, the sun arose.

Digory had never seen such a sun. You could imagine that it laughed for joy as it came up. As its beams shot across the land the travellers could see for the first time what sort of place they were in. It was a valley through which a broad, swift river wound its way, flowing eastwards towards the sun. Southward there were mountains, northward there were lower hills. But it was a valley of mere earth, rock and water; there was not a tree, not a bush, not a blade of grass to be seen. The earth was of many colours: they were fresh, hot, and vivid. They made you feel excited; until you saw the Singer himself, and then you forgot everything else.

It was a Lion. Huge, shaggy, and bright, it stood facing the risen sun. Its mouth was wide open in song and it was about three hundred yards away.

. . .

Now the song had changed. The Lion was pacing to and fro about that empty land and singing his new song. It was softer and more lilting than the song by which he had called up the stars and the sun; a gentle, rippling music. And as he walked and sang the valley grew green with grass. It spread out from the Lion like a pool. It ran up the sides of the little hills like a wave. In a few minutes it was creeping up the lower slopes of the distant mountain, making that young world every moment softer. The light wind could now be heard ruffling the grass. Soon there were other things besides grass. The higher slopes grew dark with heather. Patches of rougher and more bristling green appeared in the valley. Digory did not know what they were until one began coming up quite close to him. It was a little, spiky thing that threw out dozens of arms and covered these arms with green and grew larger at the rate of about an inch every two seconds. There were dozens of these things all round about him now. When they were nearly as tall as himself he saw what they were. "Trees!" he exclaimed.

All this time the Lion's song, and his stately prowl, to and fro, backwards and forwards, was going on. Polly was finding the song more and more interesting because she thought she was beginning to see the connection between the music and the things that were happening. When a line of dark firs sprang up on a ridge about a hundred yards away she felt that they were connected with a series of deep, prolonged notes which the Lion had sung a second before. And when he burst into a rapid series of lighter notes she was not surprised to see primroses suddenly appearing in every direction. Thus, with an unspeakable thrill, she felt quite certain that all the things were coming (as she said) 'out of the Lion's head'. When you listened to his song you heard the things he was making up: when you looked round you, you saw them. This was so exciting that she had no time to be afraid.

In a few minutes Digory came to the edge of the wood and there he stopped. The Lion was singing still. But now the song had once more changed. It was more like what we should call a tune, but it was also far wilder. It made you want to run and jump and climb. It made you want to shout. It made you want to rush at other people and either hug them or fight them. It made Digory hot and red in the face.

Can you imagine a stretch of grassy land bubbling like water in a pot? For that is really the best description of what was happening. In all directions it was swelling into humps. They were of very different sizes, some no bigger than mole-hills, some as big as wheel-barrows, two the size of cottages. And the humps moved and swelled till they burst, and the crumbled earth poured out of them, and from each hump there came out an animal. The moles came out just as you might see a mole come out in England. The dogs came out, barking the moment their heads were free, and struggling as you've seen them do when they are getting through a narrow hole in a hedge. The stags were the queerest to watch, for of course the antlers came up a long time before the rest of them, so at first Digory thought they were trees. The frogs, who all came up near the river, went straight into it with a plop-plop and loud croaking. The panthers, leopards and things of that sort, sat down at once to wash the loose earth off their hind quarters and then stood up against the trees to sharpen their front claws. Butterflies fluttered. Bees got to work on the flowers as if they hadn't a second to lose. But the greatest moment of all was when the biggest hump broke like a small earthquake and out came the sloping back, the large wise head, and the four baggy-trousered legs of an elephant. And now you could hardly hear the song of the Lion; there was so much cawing, cooing, crowing, braying, neighing, baying, barking, lowing, bleating, and trumpeting.

And now, for the first time, the Lion was quite silent. He was going to and fro among the animals. And every now and then he would go up to two of them (always two at a time) and touch their noses with his. He would touch two beavers among all the beavers, two leopards among all the leopards, one stag and one deer among all the deer, and leave the rest. Some sorts of animals he passed over altogether. But the pairs which he had touched instantly left their own kinds and followed him. At last he stood still and all the creatures whom he had touched came and stood in a wide circle around him. The others whom he had not touched began to wander away. Their noises faded gradually into the distance. The chosen beasts who remained were now utterly silent, all with their eyes fixed intently upon the Lion. The cat-like ones gave an occasional twitch of the tail but otherwise all were still. For the first time that day there was complete silence, except for the sound of running water. Digory's heart beat wildly; he knew something very solemn was going to be done.

The Lion opened his mouth, but no sound came from it; he was breathing out, a long, warm breath; it seemed to sway all the beasts as the wind sways a line of trees. Far overhead from beyond the veil of blue sky which hid them the stars sang again: a pure, cold, difficult music. Then there came a swift flash of fire (but it burnt nobody) either from the sky or from the Lion itself, and every drop of blood tingled in the children's bodies, and the deepest, wildest voice they had ever heard was saying:

"Narnia, Narnia, Narnia, awake. Love. Think. Speak. Be walking trees. Be talking beasts. Be divine waters."

From *The Magician's Nephew* by C.S. Lewis

Extract 3

The Song of the River

(In this passage the author describes a man listening to the sounds of a great river.)

Vasudeva took Siddhartha's hand, led him to the seat on the river bank, sat down beside him and smiled at the river.

'You have heard it laugh,' he said, 'but you have not heard everything. Let us listen; you will hear more.'

They listened. The many-voiced song of the river echoed softly. Siddhartha looked into the river and saw many pictures in the flowing water. ... The river's voice was sorrowful. It sang with yearning and sadness, flowing towards its goal.

'Do you hear?' asked Vasudeva's mute glance. Siddhartha nodded.

'Listen better!' whispered Vasudeva.

Siddhartha tried to listen better. The picture of his father, his own picture, and the picture of his son all flowed into each other. They all became part of the river. It was the goal of all of them, yearning, desiring, suffering; and the river's voice was full of longing, full of smarting woe, full of insatiable desire. The river flowed on towards its goal. ... The water changed to vapour and rose, became rain and came down again, became spring, brook and river, changed anew, flowed anew. But the yearning voice had altered. It still echoed sorrowfully, searchingly, but other voices accompanied it, voices of pleasure and sorrow, good and evil voices, laughing and lamenting voices, hundreds of voices, thousands of voices.

Siddhartha listened. He was now listening intently, completely absorbed, quite empty, taking in everything. He felt that he had now completely learned the art of listening. He had often heard all this before, all these numerous voices in the river, but today they sounded different. He could no longer distinguish the different voices – the merry voice from the weeping voice, the childish voice from the manly voice. They all belonged to each other: the lament of those who yearn, the laughter of the wise, the cry of indignation and groan of the dying. They were all interwoven and interlocked, entwined in a thousand ways. And all the voices, all the goals, all the yearnings, all the sorrows, all the pleasures, all the good and evil, all of them together was the world. All of them together was the stream of events, the music of life.

When Siddhartha listened attentively to this river, to this song of a thousand voices, when he did not listen to the sorrow or laughter, when he did not bind his soul to any one particular voice and absorb it in his Self, but heard them all, the whole, the unity; then the great song of a thousand voices consisted of one word: OM - perfection.

From *Siddhartha*, by Herman Hesse

Extract 4

Falling in Love with Words

The poet Dylan Thomas (1914-1953) talks about why and how he first began to write poetry.

'I should say I wanted to write poetry in the beginning because I had fallen in love with words. The first poems I knew were nursery rhymes, and before I could read them for myself I had come to love just the words of them, the words alone. What the words stood for, symbolised, or meant, was of very secondary importance; what mattered was the sound of them as I heard them for the first time on the lips of the remote and incomprehensible grown-ups who seemed, for some reason, to be living in my world. And these words were, to me, as the notes of bells, the sounds of musical instruments, the noises of wind, sea, and rain, the rattle of milkcarts, the clopping of hooves on cobbles, the fingering of branches on a window pane, might be to someone, deaf from birth, who has miraculously found his hearing. I did not care what the words said, overmuch, nor what happened to Jack and Jill and the Mother Goose rest of them; I cared for the shapes of sound that their names, and the words describing their actions, made in my ears; I cared for the colours the words cast on my eyes. I realise that I may be, as I think back all that way, romanticising my reactions to the simple and beautiful words of those pure poems; but that is all I can honestly remember, however much time might have falsified my memory. I fell in love - that is the only expression I can think of - at once, and am still at the mercy of words, though sometimes now, knowing a little of their behaviour very well, I think I can influence them slightly and have even learned to beat them now and then, which they appear to enjoy. I tumbled for words at once. And, when I began to read the nursery rhymes for myself, and, later, to read other verses and ballads, I knew that I had discovered the most important things, to me, that could be ever. There they were, seemingly lifeless, made only of black and white, but out of them, out of their own being, came love and terror and pity and pain and wonder and all the other vague abstractions that make our ephemeral lives dangerous, great and bearable. Out of them came the gusts and grunts and hiccups and heehaws of the common fun of the earth; and though what the words meant was, in its own way, often deliciously funny enough, so much funnier seemed to me, at that almost forgotten time, the shape and shade and size and noise of the words as they hummed, strummed, jigged and galloped along. That was the time of innocence; words burst upon me, unencumbered by trivial or portentous associations; words were their spring-like selves, fresh with Eden's dew, as they flew out of the air. They made their own original associations as they sprang and shone. The words, 'Ride a cock-horse to Banbury Cross', were as haunting to me, who did not know then what a cock-horse was nor cared a damn where Banbury Cross might be, as, much later, were such lines as John Donne's 'Go and catch a falling star, Get with child a mandrake root', which also I could not understand when I first read them. And as I read more and more, and it was not all verse, by any means, my love for the real life of words increased until I knew that I must live with them and in them, always. I knew, in fact, that I must be a writer of words, and nothing else. The first thing was to feel and know their sound and substance; what I was going to do with those words, what use I was going to make of them, would come later. I knew I had to know them most intimately in all their forms and moods, their ups and downs, their chops and changes, their needs and demands. (Here, I am afraid, I am beginning to talk too vaguely. I do not like writing about words, because then I often use bad and wrong and stale and woolly words. What I like to do is to treat words as a craftsman does his wood or stone or what-have-you, to hew, carve, mould, coil, polish and plane them into patterns, sequences, sculptures, fugues of sound expressing some lyrical impulse, some spiritual doubt or conviction, some dimly realised truth I must try to reach and realise.) It was when I was very young, and just at school, that, in my father's study, before homework that was never done, I began to know one kind of writing from another, one kind of goodness, one kind of badness. My first, and greatest, liberty was that of being able to read everything and anything I cared to. I read indiscriminately, and with my eyes hanging out. I could never have dreamt that there were such goings-on in the world between the covers of books, such slashing of humbug, and humbug too, such staggering peace, such enormous laughter, such sand-storms and ice-blasts of words, such and so many blinding bright lights breaking across the just-awaking wits and splashing all over the pages in a million bits and pieces all of which were words, words, words, and each of which was alive forever in its own delight and glory and oddity and light.'

Appendix B – The Changing Language

1. Sanskrit

Geeta Ch. 13 verses 29–34

प्रकृत्यैव च कर्माणि क्रियमाणानि सर्वशः ।
यः पश्यति तथात्मानमकर्तारं स पश्यति ॥२९

यदा भूतपृथग्भावमेकस्थमनुपश्यति ।
तत एव च विस्तारं ब्रह्म संपद्यते तदा ॥३०

अनादित्वान्निर्गुणत्वात्परमात्मायमव्ययः ।
शरीरस्थोऽपि कौन्तेय न करोति न लिप्यते ॥३१

यथा सर्वगतं सौक्ष्म्यादाकाशं नोपलिप्यते ।
सर्वत्रावस्थितो देहे तथात्मा नोपलिप्यते ॥३२

यथा प्रकाशयत्येकः कृत्स्नंलोकमिमं रविः ।
क्षेत्रं क्षेत्री तथा कृत्स्नं प्रकाशयति भारत ॥३३

क्षेत्रक्षेत्रज्ञयोरेवमन्तरं ज्ञानचक्षुषा ।
भूतप्रकृतिमोक्षं च ये विदुर्यान्ति ते परम् ॥३४

He who understands that it is only the Law of Nature that brings action to fruition, and that the Self never acts, alone knows the Truth.
He who sees the diverse forms of life all rooted in the One, and growing forth from Him, he shall indeed find the Absolute.
The Supreme Spirit, O Prince! is without beginning, without Qualities and Imperishable, and though it be within the body, yet It does not act, nor is It affected by action.
As space, though present everywhere, remains by reason of its subtlety unaffected, so the Self, though present in all forms, retains its purity unalloyed.
As the one Sun illuminates the whole earth, so the Lord illumines the whole universe.
Those who with the eye of wisdom thus see the difference between Matter and Spirit, and know how to liberate Life from the Law of Nature, they attain the Supreme.

2. Greek

ἄνδρα μοι ἔννεπε, μοῦσα, πολύτροπον, ὃς μάλα πολλὰ
πλάγχθη, ἐπεὶ Τροίης ἱερὸν πτολίεθρον ἔπερσεν.
πολλῶν δ' ἀνθρώπων ἴδεν ἄστεα καὶ νόον ἔγνω,
πολλὰ δ' ὅ γ' ἐν πόντῳ πάθεν ἄλγεα ὃν κατὰ θυμόν,
5   ἀρνύμενος ἥν τε ψυχὴν καὶ νόστον ἑταίρων.
ἀλλ' οὐδ' ὣς ἑτάρους ἐρρύσατο, ἱέμενός περ·
αὐτῶν γὰρ σφετέρῃσιν ἀτασθαλίῃσιν ὄλοντο,
νήπιοι, οἳ κατὰ βοῦς Ὑπερίονος Ἠελίοιο
ἤσθιον· αὐτὰρ ὁ τοῖσιν ἀφείλετο νόστιμον ἦμαρ.
10 τῶν ἁμόθεν γε, θεά, θύγατερ Διός, εἰπὲ καὶ ἡμῖν.
ἔνθ' ἄλλοι μὲν πάντες, ὅσοι φύγον αἰπὺν ὄλεθρον,
οἴκοι ἔσαν, πόλεμόν τε πεφευγότες ἠδὲ θάλασσαν·
τὸν δ' οἶον νόστου κεχρημένον ἠδὲ γυναικὸς
νύμφη πότνι' ἔρυκε Καλυψὼ δῖα θεάων
15 ἐν σπέσσι γλαφυροῖσι, λιλαιομένη πόσιν εἶναι.
ἀλλ' ὅτε δὴ ἔτος ἦλθε περιπλομένων ἐνιαυτῶν,
τῷ οἱ ἐπεκλώσαντο θεοὶ οἶκόνδε νέεσθαι
εἰς Ἰθάκην, οὐδ' ἔνθα πεφυγμένος ἦεν ἀέθλων
καὶ μετὰ οἷσι φίλοισι. θεοὶ δ' ἐλέαιρον ἅπαντες
20 νόσφι Ποσειδάωνος· ὁ δ' ἀσπερχὲς μενέαινεν
ἀντιθέῳ Ὀδυσῆι πάρος ἣν γαῖαν ἱκέσθαι.

The hero of the tale which I beg the Muse to help me tell is that resourceful man who roamed the wide world after he had sacked the holy citadel of Troy. He saw the cities of many peoples and he learnt their ways. He suffered many hardships on the high seas in his struggles to preserve his life and bring his comrades home. But he failed to save those comrades, in spite of all his efforts. It was their own sin that brought them to their doom, for in their folly they devoured the oxen of Hyperion the Sun, and the god saw to it that they should never return. This is the tale I pray the divine Muse to unfold to us. Begin it, goddess, at whatever point you will.

All the survivors of the war had reached their homes by now and so put the perils of battle and the sea behind them. Odysseus alone was prevented from returning to the home and wife he longed for by that powerful goddess, the Nymph Calypso, who wished him to marry her, and kept him in her vaulted cave. Not even when the rolling seasons brought in the year which the gods had chosen for his homecoming to Ithaca was he clear of his troubles and safe among his friends. Yet all the gods were sorry for him, except Poseidon, who pursued the heroic Odysseus with relentless malice till the day when he reached his own country.

From The Odyssey *of Homer*

3. Latin

Arma virumque cano, Troiae qui primus ab oris
Italiam, fato profugus, Laviniaque venit
litora, multum ille et terris iactatus et alto
vi superum saevae memorem Iunonis ob iram;
multa quoque et bello passus, dum conderet urbem,
inferretque deos Latio, genus unde Latinum
Albanique patres, atque altae moenia Romae.

Musa, mihi causas memora, quo numine laeso,
quidve dolens, regina deum tot volvere casus
insignem pietate virum, tot adire labores
impulerit. Tantaene animis caelestibus irae?

Urbs antiqua fuit, Tyrii tenuere coloni,
Karthago, Italiam contra Tiberinaque longe
ostia, dives opum studiisque asperrima belli;
quam Iuno fertur terris magis omnibus unam
posthabita coluisse Samo; hic illius arma,
hic currus fuit; hoc regnum dea gentibus esse,
si qua fata sinant, iam tum tenditque fovetque.
Progeniem sed enim Troiano a sanguine duci
audierat, Tyrias olim quae verteret arces;
hinc populum late regem belloque superbum
venturum excidio Libyae: sic volvere Parcas.

This is a tale of arms and of a man. Fated to be an exile, he was the first to sail from the land of Troy and reach Italy, at its Lavinian shore. He met many tribulations on his way both by land and on the ocean; high Heaven willed it, for Juno was ruthless and could not forget her anger. And he had also to endure great suffering in warfare. But at last he succeeded in founding his city, and installing the gods of his race in the Latin land: and that was the origin of the Latin nation, the Lords of Alba, and the proud battlements of Rome.

I pray for inspiration, to tell how it all began, and how the Queen of Heaven sustained such outrage to her majesty that in her indignation she forced a man famed for his true-heartedness to tread that long path of adventure, and to face so many trials. It is hard to believe gods in heaven capable of such rancour.

Once there was an ancient town called Carthage, inhabited by emigrants from Tyre, and confronting Italy, opposite to the mouth of the Tiber but far away. Carthage had wealth and power; and it had skill and ferocity in war. Now Juno is said to have loved Carthage best of all cities in the world, giving even Samos the second place. She kept her weapons and her chariot there; and she had already set her heart on making it a capital city governing all the earth, and spared no effort of fostering care, hoping that Destiny might consent to her desire. She had, however, heard of another breed of men, tracing descent from the blood of Troy, who were one day to overthrow this Tyrian stronghold; for they would breed a warrior nation, haughty, and sovereign over wide realms; and their onset would bring destruction to Africa. Such, she had heard, was the plan of the spinning Fates.

From The Aeneid *of Virgil*

4. Anglo-Saxon, or Old English

Pronunciation of Old English

Anglo-Saxon has some letters which are no longer part of our modern English alphabet. They are called runic letters. Runes are magical verses, used as magic charms to protect one from evil. The idea is that language contains a mystery which only the wise can understand. There are four runic letters used in Anglo-Saxon literature. They are:

ash – æ; thorn – þ; yogh – ʒ; 'bar-d' or eth – ð

Stress: In Anglo-Saxon, where the word has more than one syllable, the stress usually falls on the first one. An exception to this is the prefix ge – which is always unstressed – gebiden.

Sounds: Here, first, are the Anglo-Saxon vowel sounds

æ	sæt	as in MnE *sat*	ǣ	dǣd	as in French *bête*
a	mann	as in American *hot*	ā	hām	as in MnE *father*
i	sittan	as in MnE *sit*	ī	wīd	as in MnE *weed*
u	ful	as in MnE *full*	ū	hūs	as in MnE *goose*
e	settan	as in MnE *set*	ē	hē	as in German *Leben*
o	God	as in MnE *God*	ō	gōd	as in German *Sohn*
	before a nasal (m, n, ng) – e.g. monn – as American *hot*				
y	wynn	as in French *tu*	ȳ	rȳman	as in French *ruse*

All the vowels in unstressed syllables are pronounced clearly, except final e.

The language is full of diphthongs (dual vowel sounds) such as *heold*, *eall*, etc. Both vowels in a diphthong are sounded, but as a single syllable (i.e. not as in modern English meat, field – in Old English these would be pronounced 'mayat' and 'fee-eld' spoken as a single syllable).

And here are the consonant sounds:

þ = th   ð = th (ð not used as initial letter)   ʒ = y or g

All consonants are pronounced. There are no 'silent letters' e.g. *cnapa, gnæt, hlaf, writan*

Double consonants. A little 'timegap' is allowed for the second consonant – *bid-dan* (you can hear the difference this makes if you compare 'reddish' (colour) with 'red dish'.)

s, f, þ, ð – when between vowels or voiced sounds – are *voiced*. i.e. as z, v, <u>th</u> *risan, heofen, paþas, hæfde*.

Otherwise voiceless: *sittan, hlaf, paþ*. (cf modern English loaf, loaves, path, paths)

h – initially as *hat*. Otherwise as Scots *loch*. e.g. *niht*.

c – as hard k before a o u or y, but usually ch before i or e

g – as hard g before a o u or y, but as soft y before i or e

sc = sh *scip* (ship)

cg = dge *ecg* (edge)

Extract 1

Cædmon's Hymn

Nū wē sculon heriʒean   heofonrīces Weard
Now we should praise   the Ruler of heaven,
Meotodes meahte   ond his mōdgeþanc
Maker's might,   and the thought of his mind,
weorc Wuldorfæder   swā hē wundra gehwæs
Work of the glorious father,   so wondrous he was,
ēce Drihten   ōr onstealde
eternal Lord,   he established the beginning.
Hē ǣrest sceōp   eorðan bearnum
He first created   for the children of earth
heofon tō hrōfe   hālig Scyppend
the heaven as a roof,   holy Creator.
Þā middangeard   monncynnes Weard
Then middle earth   the Ruler of mankind,
ēce Drihten   æfter tēode
eternal Lord,   afterwards adorned
fīrum foldan   Frēa ælmihtig.
the earth for men,   almighty God.

Extract 2

The Wanderer

'Oft him ānhaga   āre gebīdeð
Often the solitary one   longs for grace,
Metudes miltse   þēah þe hē mōdcearig
Maker's mercy   yet troubled in mind
geond lagulāde   longe sceolde
through the sea's tract   he must for long
hrēran mid hondum   hrīmcealde sǣ,
stir with hands   the ice-cold sea,
wadan wrǣclastas: wyrd bið ful ārǣd.'
travel the paths of exile: wyrd is set fast.'
Swā cwæð eardstapa   earfeþa gemyndig.
Thus speaks the wanderer,   mindful of hardships.

Extract 3

The Battle of Maldon

'Hige sceal þē heardre,   heorte þē cēnre,
Mind shall be the harder,   heart the keener,
mōd sceal þē māre,   þē ūre mægen lȳtlað.
Courage the greater,   as our strength grows less.
Hēr līð ūre ealdor   eall forhēawen,
Here lies our lord   all hewn down
gōd on grēote;   ā mæg gnornian
good man in the dust;   ever may he mourn
sē ðē nū fram þīs wīgplegan   wenden þenceð.
who now from this battle-play   thinks to wend.
Ic eom frōd fēores.   Fram ic ne wille,
I am advanced in life.   I will not go away
ac ic mē be healfe   mīnum hlāforde
But I by the side   of my lord
be swā lēofan men   licgan þence.'
beside the man so loved   I think to lie.

Extract 4

See if you can translate this passage with the help of the glossary that follows on pages 44–45. It was originally written to teach young boys Latin. They had to translate this little play into Latin from the English they spoke at that time.

Ælfric's Colloquy

The Ploughman

Master: Hwæt sæʒst þū, Yrþling; hū begǣst þū þīn weorc?

Ploughman: Ēalā, lēof hlāford, þearle ic deorfe; ic gā ūt on dægrǣd, þȳwende oxan tō felda, and ʒeocie hi to sȳl; nys hyt swā stearc winter þæt ic durre lūtian æt hām, for mīnes hlāfordes eʒe; ac ge-ʒeocodum oxum, and gefæstnodum sceare and cultre mid þǣre syl, ælce dæg ic sceal erian fulne æcer oþþe māre.

Master: Hæfst þū ǣnige gefēran?

Ploughman: Ic hæbbe sumne cnapan þȳwende oxan mid gād-īsene, þe ēac swylce nū hās ys, for cylde and hrēame.

Master: Hwæt māre dēst þū on dæg?

Ploughman: Gewislice þænne māre ic do. Ic sceal fyllan oxena binna mid hiʒ, and wæterian hiʒ and beran ūt heora scearn.

Master: Hiʒ, hiʒ, micel gedeorf ys hit!

Ploughman: Ʒea, lēof, micel gedeorf hit ys, forþān ic neom frēoh.

The Shepherd and the Neat-herd

Master: Hwæt sæʒst þū, Scēap-hyrde? Hæfst þū ǣnig gedeorf?

Shepherd: Ʒea, lēof, ic hæbbe; on foreweardne morʒen ic drīfe mīne scēap tō heora lǣse, and stande ofer hiʒ, on hǣte an on cyle, mid hundum, þē-lǣs wulfas forswelʒen hiʒ, and ic āʒen lǣde hiʒ tō heora locum, and melce hiʒ tweowa on dæg, and heora locu ic hebbe þærto, and cȳse and buteran ic do, and ic eaom getrȳwe hlāforde mīnum.

Master: Ēalā, Oxan-hyrde, hwæt wyrcst þū?

Neat-herd: Ēalā, min hlāford, micel ic gedeorfe; þænne se yrþling unscenþ þā oxan, ic lǣde hī to lǣse, and ealle niht ic stande ofer hī waciende for þēofum, and eft, on ærne merʒen, ic betǣce hī þam yrþlinge, wel gefylde and gewæterode.

The Hunter

Master: Canst þū ǣnig þing?

Hunter: Ǣnne cræft ic cann.

Master: Hwylcne?

Hunter: Hunta ic eom.

Master: Hwæs?

Hunter: Cyninges.

Master: Hū begǣst þū þīnne cræft?

Hunter: Ic breȝde mē max, and sette hī on gehæppre stōwe and getihte mīne hundas, þæt hī ēhton wilddēor, oþ þæt þe hī cumen to þām nettum unforsceawodlīce, þæt hī swa beon begrynode, and ic ofslēah hī on þām maxum.

Master: Ne canst þū huntian būton miol nettum?

Hunter: Ȝea, būtan nettum huntian ic mæg.

Master: Hū?

Hunter: Mid swiftum hundum ic becǣce wilddēor.

Master: Hwylce wilddēor swȳþost gefēhst þū?

Hunter: Ic gefō heortas, and bāras, and rāan, and rǣȝan, and hwīlum haran.

Master: Wǣre þū tō dæg on huntnoðe?

Hunter: Ic næs forþān sunnan dæg ys, ac ȝiestrandæg ic wæs on huntunge.

Master: Hwæt gelǣhtest þū?

Hunter: Twēgen heortas and ǣnne bār.

Master: Hū gefēngc þū hī?

Hunter: Heortas ic gefēng on nettum, and bār ic ofslōh.

Master: Hū wǣre þū þrȳstiȝ ofstician bār?

Hunter: Hundas bedrīfon hine tō mē, and ic þǣr, tōgēanes standende, fǣrlīce ofsticode hine.

Glossary

yrþling	ploughman	þe-læs	lest, in case
bēgan	to perform	for-swelgan	to swallow
begæst	you (thou) perform	hundum	dogs
lēof	beloved, dear	locum	sheepfold
hlāford	lord	locu	bars, bolt
þearle	greatly	melcan	to milk
ic	I	heora	their
deorfan	to labour, work	hebbe	lift, raise
gān	to go	getrȳwe	true
dægræd	'dayred' – dawn	læse	pasture
þȳwan	to drive	waciende	watching
þȳwende	driving	þēofum	thieves
ac	but	eft	afterwards
ȝeocian	to yoke	ærne	early
ge-ȝeocodum	yoked	betæce	take
sȳl	plough	cyning	king
nys (ne is)	is not	breȝdan	weave
durran	to dare	max	net
lūtian	to lurk	gehæp	suitable
sceare	ploughshare	stōwe	place
cultre	coulter (blade)	getihan	to incite
mid	with	ēhtan	to pursue
ǣlce	each	oþ þæt þe	until
erian	to plough	unforsceawodlīce	unexpectedly
oþþe māre	up to as much as	begrynian	to ensnare
gefēran	companion, comrade	ofslēan	to slay, kill
cnapa	boy	būton	without
gād-īsen	goad	becæcan	to catch
þe	who	wilddēor	animals
ēac swycle	besides, also	swȳþost	most
nū	now	gefēhst	take
hās	hoarse	heortas	stags
hrēam	shouting	bāras	boars
gewislice	certainly	rāan	roe-deer
hiȝ	hay/them	ræȝan	she-goats
hiȝ hiȝ	heigh ho	hwīlum	sometimes
scearn	dung	gelæhtest	caught
micel	much, a lot	gefēnge	took
gedeorf	labour, work	ofslōh	killed
forþān	therefore, so	þrȳstiȝ	bold
neom (ne eom)	am not	ofstician	to stab to death
frēoh	free	bedrīfon	drove
hæbbe	have	tōgēanes	in wait
foreweard	early	fǣrlīce	suddenly

5. Middle English

Extract 1

From The Franklin's Tale by Geoffrey Chaucer (1343–1400)

(This is written in the so-called 'London dialect' from which modern English has developed.)

In Armorik, that called is Britaine,	Armorik: *Armorica, the old name for Brittany*
Ther was a knight that loved and dide his paine	
To serve a lady in his beste wise;	in his best wise: *in the best way he could*
And many a labour, many a greet emprise	emprise: *undertaking*
He for his lady wroghte, er she were wonne.	er: *before*
For she was oon the faireste under sonne,	*one who was the fairest upon earth*
And eek thereto comen of so heigh kinrede	eek: *also* so heigh kinrede*: such noble kin*
That wel unnethes dorste this knight, for drede,	unnethes: *hardly*
Telle hire his wo, his peyne, and his distresse.	
But atte laste she, for his worthinesse,	
And namely for his meke obeisaunce,	namely: *in particular*
Hath swich a pitee caught of his penaunce	*took such pity on his suffering*
That prively she fil of his accord	prively: *secretly*
To take him for hir housbonde and hir lord,	
Of swich lordshipe as men han over hir wives.	han: *have*

Extract 2

From Sir Gawain and the Green Knight
(anonymous, 14th century)

*(This is written in the West Midlands dialect, and is closer to Anglo-Saxon.
See if you can understand it)*

'Nay, as help me,' quod þe haþel, 'he þat on hyȝe syttes,	haþel: *man* syttes: *dwells*
To wone any quyle in þis won, hit watz not myn ernde;	wone: *stay*
	quyle: *while*
Bot for þe los of þe, lede, is lyft vp so hyȝe,	ernde: *errand* los: *praise*
	lede: *prince*
And þy burȝ and þy burnes best ar holden,	burȝ: *(burgh) castle* burnes: *knights*
Stifest vnder stel-gere on stedes to ryde,	stifest: *strongest* stele-gere: *armour*
Þe wyȝtest and þe worþyest of þe worldes kynde,	on stedes: *on horseback*
	wyȝtest: *bravest*
Preue for to play wyth in oþer pure laykez,	preue: *valiant* pure laykez: *noble sports*

And here is kydde cortaysye, as I haf herd carp,   kydde: *shown* carp: *tell*
And þat hatz wayned me hider, iwyis, at þis tyme.   wayned: *brought* iwyis: *indeed*

Extract 3

From The Cloud of Unknowing
(anonymous 14th century)

Look up now, weike wreche, & see what þou arte. What arte þou, & what
hast þou deserued, þus to be clepid of oure Lorde? What weri wrechid herte
& sleping in sleuþe is þat, þe whiche is not waknid wiþ þe drawȝt of þis
loue & þe voise of þis cleping?

clepid: *called* weri: *weary* sleuþe: *sloth* drawȝt: *drawing* cleping: *calling*

Extract 4

From the prologue to The Canterbury Tales
by Geoffrey Chaucer (1343–1400)

Whan that Aprill with his shoures soote	*sweet showers*
The droghte of March hath perced to the roote,	*drought pierced*
And bathed every veine in swich licour	*such moisture*
Of which vertu engendred is the flour;	vertu: *creative power*
Whan Zephirus eek with his sweete breeth	Zephirus: *the West Wind*
Inspired hath in every holt and heeth	holt: *copse*
The tendre croppes and the yonge sonne	
Hath in the Ram his have cours yronne,	*has half run his course in Aries*
And smale foweles maken melodie,	foweles: *birds*
That slepen al the night with open ye	ye: *eye*
(So priketh hem nature in hir corages);	*so strongly nature stimulates their desires*
Thanne longen folk to goon on pilgrimages,	
And palmeres for to seken straunge strondes,	strondes: *shores*
To ferne halwes, kowthe in sondry londes;	ferne: *distant* halwes: *shrines*
	kowthe: *known*
And specially from every shires ende	
Of Engelond to Caunterbury they wende,	wende: *go*
The hooly blisful martir for to seke,	
That hem hath holpen whan that they were seeke.	seeke: *sick*

Try reciting it together, using the pronunciation guide on the next page.

Pronunciation Guide

Short Vowels

a, as *u* in 'cut'

e, as in 'set'

i, as in 'is'

o, as in 'top'

u as in 'put'

final *e* is a neutral sound like the first syllable of 'about', and is always sounded unless the next word begins with a vowel or an *h*.

Long Vowels

ā as in 'car'

ē as in 'take' or 'there'

ī as in 'machine'

ō as *aw* in 'fawn' or as in 'note'

ū as in French *tu*

Diphthongs

ai and *ei*, as sound 'y' in 'sky'

au and *aw* as sound 'ow' in 'now' or 'house'

ou and *ow* – either as sound 'ou' in 'through', or as sound 'ou' in 'mouse'

Consonants

Mostly as Modern English, but without 'silent' consonants.

gh as 'ch' in Scottish 'loch'.

Both consonants sounded in *kn*ave, *gn*acchen, wo*rd*, fo*lk*, *wr*ong.

6. Renaissance English

Extract 1

Sir Thomas More's Farewell (1557)
(written from his cell in the Tower of London
just before his death)

Oure Lorde blesse you, good doughter, and youre good housbande, and youre lyttle boye, and all yours, and all my chyldren and all my Goddechyldren and all our frendes. Recommende me when ye maye, to my good doughter Cicily, whom I beseche oure Lorde to coumforte. And I sende her my blessyng, and to all her children, and praye her to praye for me. I sende her an handkercher: and God coumfort my good sonne her husbande. My good doughter Daunce hathe the picture in parchemente, that you delyvered me from my ladye Coniers, her name is on the backeside. Shew her that I hartelye praye her, that you may sende it in my name to her agayne, for a token from me to praye for me. I lyke speciall wel Dorothy Coly, I pray you be good unto her. I woulde wytte whether thys be she that you wrote me of. If not yet I praye you bee good to the tother, as you maye in her affliccion, and to my good doughter Joone Aleyn too. Geve her I praye you some kynde aunswere, for she sued hither to me this day to pray you be good to her. I comber you good Margaret much, but I would be sory, if it should be any lenger than tomorow. For it is saint Thomas even, and the utas [*octave*] of saint Peter: and therefore tomorow long I to go to God: it were a day verye mete and convenient for me. I never liked your maner toward me better, than when you kissed me laste: for I love when doughterly love and deere charitye hath no laysure to loke to worldlye curtesy. Fare well my dere chylde, and pray for me, and I shall for you and all youre frendes, that we may merelye mete in heaven. I thank you for youre gret cost. I sende now to my good doughter Clement her algorisme stone [*counter*], and I send her and my godsonne and all hers, Gods blessing and myne. I praye you at time convenient recomende me to my good sonne John More I liked wel his naturall fashion. Our Lord blesse hym and his good wyfe my lovyng doughter, to whom I praye him be good as he hathe greate cause: and that yf the lande of myne come to hande, he break not my wyll concernynge hys sister Daunce. And oure Lord blisse Thomas and Austen and all that they shal have.

Extract 2

From **The Book of Common Prayer** *(1662)*

Almighty God, Father of our Lord Jesus Christ, Maker of all things, Judge of all men; We acknowledge and bewail our manifold sins and wickedness, Which we, from time to time, most grievously have committed, By thought, word and deed, Against thy Divine Majesty, Provoking most justly thy wrath and indignation against us. We do earnestly repent, and are heartily sorry for these our misdoings; The remembrance of them is grievous unto us; The burden of them is intolerable. Have mercy upon us, Have mercy upon us, most merciful Father; For thy Son our Lord Jesus Christ's sake, Forgive us all that is past; and grant that we may ever hereafter Serve and please thee In newness of life, To the honour and glory of thy Name; Through Jesus Christ our Lord. Amen.

Extract 3

From **The Authorized Version of the Bible** *(1611)*

Take no thought for your life, what ye shall eat, or what ye shall drink; nor yet for your body, what ye shall put on. Is not the life more than meat, and the body than raiment?
Behold the fowls of the air: for they sow not, neither do they reap, nor gather into barns; yet your heavenly Father feedeth them. Are ye not much better than they? Which of you by taking thought can add one cubit unto his stature?
And why take ye thought for raiment? Consider the lilies of the field, how they grow; they toil not, neither do they spin;
And yet I say unto you, that even Solomon in all his glory was not arrayed like one of these.
Wherefore, if God so clothe the grass of the field, which today is, and tomorrow is cast into the oven, shall he not much more clothe you, O ye of little faith?
Therefore take no thought, saying, What shall we eat? or, What shall we drink? or, Wherewithal shall we be clothed?
(For after all these things do the Gentiles seek); for your heavenly Father knoweth that ye have need of all these things.
But seek ye first the kingdom of God, and his righteousness; and all these things shall be added unto you.
Take therefore no thought for the morrow; for the morrow shall take thought for the things of itself. Sufficient unto the day is the evil thereof.

St Matthew, Chapter VI, verses 25–34

Extract 4

From **The Merchant of Venice** *(c. 1595)*

How sweet the moonlight sleeps upon this bank!
Here will we sit and let the sounds of music
Creep in our ears; soft stillness and the night
Become the touches of sweet harmony.
Sit, Jessica. Look how the floor of heaven
Is thick inlaid with patines of bright gold;
There's not the smallest orb which thou behold'st
But in his motion like an angel sings,
Still quiring to the young-ey'd cherubins;
Such harmony is in immortal souls,
But whilst this muddy vesture of decay
Doth grossly clothe it in, we cannot hear it.

William Shakespeare (1564–1616)

7. Modern English

Extract 1

The Telephone Call

Please, God, let him telephone me now. Dear God, let him call me now. I won't ask anything else of You, truly I won't. It isn't very much to ask. It would be so little to You, God, such a little, little thing. Only let him telephone now. Please, God. Please, please, please.

If I didn't think about it, maybe the telephone might ring. Sometimes it does that. If I could think of something else. If I could think of something else. Maybe if I counted five hundred by fives, it might ring by that time. I'll count slowly. I won't cheat. And if it rings when I get to three hundred, I won't stop; I won't answer it until I get to five hundred. Five, ten, fifteen, twenty, twenty-five, thirty, thirty-five, forty, forty-five, fifty.... Oh, please ring. Please.

This is the last time I'll look at the clock. I will not look at it again. It's ten minutes past seven. He said he would telephone at five o'clock. "I'll call you at five, darling." I think that's where he said "darling". I'm almost sure he said it there. I know he called me "darling" twice, and the other time was when he said good-bye. "Good-bye, darling." He was busy, and he can't say much in the office, but he called me "darling" twice. He couldn't have minded my calling him up. I know you shouldn't keep telephoning them – I know they don't like that. When you do that, they know you are thinking about them and wanting them, and that makes them hate you. But I hadn't talked to him in three days – not in three days. And all I did was ask him how he was; it was just the way anybody might have called him up. He couldn't have minded that. He couldn't have thought I was bothering him. "No, of course you're not," he said. And he said he'd telephone me. He didn't have to say that. I didn't ask him to, truly I didn't. I'm sure I didn't. I don't think he would say he'd telephone me, and then just never do it. Please don't let him do that, God. Please don't.

Dorothy Parker (1893–1967)

Extract 2

From **Oleanna** *by David Mamet (1992)*

(This play is set in an American university. There are just two characters. John is a university professor. Carol is one of his students. The term 'real estate' in the USA means 'property' – i.e. houses – and a 'realtor' is an estate agent.)

Scene One. JOHN is talking on the phone. CAROL is seated across the desk from him.

JOHN *(on phone)* And what about the land. *(Pause)* The land. And what about the land? *(Pause)* What about it? *(Pause)* No. I don't understand. Well, yes, I'm I'm... no, I'm sure it's signif... I'm sure it's significant. *(Pause)* Because it's significant to mmmmmmm... did you call Jerry? *(Pause)* Because... no, no, no, no, no. What did they say...? Did you speak to the real estate... where is she...? Well, well, all right. Where are her notes? Where are the notes we took with her. *(Pause)* I thought you were? No. No, I'm sorry, I didn't mean that, I just thought that I saw you, when we were there... what...? I thought I saw you with a pencil. WHY NOW? is what I'm say... well, that's why I say "call Jerry". Well, I can't right now, be... no, I didn't schedule any... Grace: I didn't... I'm well aware... Look: Look. Did you call Jerry? Because I can't now. I'll be there, I'm sure I'll be there in fifteen, in twenty. I intend to. No, we aren't going to lose the, we aren't going to lose the house. Look: Look, I'm not minimising it. The "easement". Did she say "easement"? *(Pause)* What did she say; is it a "term of art", are we bound by it... I'm sorry... *(Pause)* are: we: yes. Bound by... Look: *(He checks his watch.)* before the other side goes home, all right? "a term of art." Because: that's right *(Pause)* The yard for the boy. Well, that's the whole... Look: I'm going to meet you there... *(He checks his watch.)* Is the realtor there? All right, tell her to show you the basement again. Look at the this because... Bec... I'm leaving in, I'm leaving in ten or fifteen... Yes. No, no, I'll meet you in the new... That a good. If he thinks it's nec... you tell Jerry to meet... All right? We aren't going to lose the deposit. All right? I'm sure it's going to be... *(Pause)* I hope so. *(Pause)* I love you too. As soon as... I will.

(He hangs up. He bends over the desk and makes a note. He looks up. To CAROL:) I'm sorry.
CAROL: *(Pause)* What is a "term of art"?
JOHN: *(Pause)* I'm sorry...?
CAROL: *(Pause)* What is a "term of art"?
JOHN: Is that what you want to talk about?
CAROL: ... to talk about...?
JOHN: Let's take the mysticism out of it, shall we? Carol? *(Pause)* Don't you think? I'll tell you: when you have some "thing". Which must be broached. *(Pause)* Don't you think...? *(Pause)*
CAROL: ... don't I think...?
JOHN: Mmm?
CAROL: ... did I...?
JOHN: ... what?
CAROL: Did... did I... did I say something wr...
JOHN: *(Pause)* No. I'm sorry. No. You're right. I'm very sorry. I'm somewhat rushed. As you see. I'm sorry. You're right. *(Pause)* What is a "term of art"? It seems to mean a term, which has come, through its use, to mean something more specific than the words would, to someone not acquainted with them... indicate. That, I believe, is what a "term of art" would mean. *(Pause)*
CAROL: You don't know what it means...?

Extract 3

From The Independent *(16th February 2000)*

Are Men the New Women?

I'm writing this piece in my cornflower blue office, typing it out on my baby-blue iMac, a machine that looks as though it were designed to be used in a hair-dresser's or a beauty parlour. At lunch, I'll probably nip round the corner, to one of the female-friendly designer restaurants that line Bond Street (you know the kind of thing, ergonomically acceptable furniture, Phalaenopsis orchids, condiments in silly pastel colours and sandwiches and salads bereft of anything approaching red meat). Later, I'll drive home in my Mercedes, a legendary car with unnecessarily girlish tendencies – like most cars these days, particularly the smaller ones, it comes complete with gentle curves, soft textures and feminine-looking lights; obviously I didn't choose a babyish, bubblegum colour such as yellow or orange, but then I wouldn't, would I? After all, I'm a man.

Later still, I might pop into a bar in Soho, one of those that actively encourage women in packs, and be served some strange-coloured Ladyboy drink in a funny glass. If I make it to the cinema I'll no doubt be forced to sit through something in which Diane Keaton or Julia Roberts, or even Madonna these days, has some kind of off-on relationship with a gay man, usually played by Greg Kinnear or Rupert Everett, before discovering the virtues of female bonding, sitting with their knees tucked up to their chin, holding warm beverages with both hands. (The three scariest words in cinema history? 'Starring Meg Ryan.') And if I fall asleep in front of the television later I'll no doubt be woken by the screams of some hapless man being made to look stupid in a commercial for anything from a car or mobile phone to a power drill or a detergent. Seems like we're living in a feminised world.

So, are men really the new women, or are we just getting soft? Everywhere you look these days we see the complete feminisation of men. All types of cars are now designed for women, as are shops (retail environments), drinks (Malibu anyone, or an Archer's?), bars, films, cinemas, bookstores, ironmongers, even sex shops. Anything that one might once have considered to be a male domain has now been subsumed by women. Caveman, it seems, has now been turned into quiche man.

Can we have our ball back, please?

Please?

Dylan Jones, Editor of 'GQ' Magazine